SKILLS FOR LAWYERS

SKILLS FOR LAWYERS

Deborah L Green LLB (Warwick), Solicitor

John Holtam LLB (Southampton), Solicitor

Priscilla Sarton LLM (London), Solicitor

Susan Scorey BA, PGCE, ALA

Gemma M Shield LLB (Hons), Solicitor

Allun Thomas LLB (London), Solicitor

JORDANS

2000

Published by
Jordan Publishing Limited
21 St Thomas Street
Bristol BS1 6JS

© The College of Law 2000

All rights reserved. No part of this publication may be
reproduced, stored in a retrieval system, or transmitted in
any way or by any means, including photocopying or recording,
without the written permission of the copyright holder,
application for which should be addressed to the publisher.

British Library Cataloguing-in-Publication Data
A catalogue record for this book is available from the British Library.

ISSN 1353–6648
ISBN 0 85308 661 3

Printed in Great Britain by Hobbs The Printers Ltd of Southampton

PREFACE

Knowledge of how the internal combustion engine works and what the Highway Code states does not necessarily make a good driver. In the same way, knowledge of the law does not necessarily make a good lawyer. The practice of law requires not merely an understanding of law and procedure but also the skills necessary to utilise that knowledge effectively.

The purpose of this Resource Book is to help prospective practitioners to develop fundamental skills which will prove essential in their later careers. Those skills are as follows:

(1) writing and drafting;
(2) legal research;
(3) interviewing and advising clients;
(4) negotiation; and
(5) advocacy.

The chapters covering each of these skills are essential preparatory reading for practice of the relevant skill on the Legal Practice Course. It is hoped that they will also prove useful in later years for the trainee or qualified solicitor, both to monitor one's own development and to evaluate others, learning from their successes and their failures.

Thanks are due to authors of the constituent Parts in earlier editions for originating and developing various chapters. They are:

Part I   Rachel Hawes
Part II   Carol Moore, Alison Baigent, Ian Cross, Stephen Sellers and Joanne Tomlinson
Part III   Martin Iller, Peter Mott

Needless to say, the current team of authors bears responsibility for any failings in this edition.

The origins of Part III lie in a series of Professional Development courses which The College of Law ran for the solicitors' profession for a number of years. In mounting the interviewing and negotiating courses, the College received invaluable assistance from Dr Karl Mackie (now Chief Executive of the Centre for Dispute Resolution). Similarly, the courses on advocacy benefited greatly from the advice and help of His Honour Judge Groves, Her Honour Judge Marian Norrie, His Honour Judge Nigel Fricker QC and Tony Edwards, solicitor. In addition, we would wish to express our gratitude to the many solicitors who attended the courses and contributed their know-how to them, and consequently to these chapters.

CONTENTS

PREFACE		v
PART I	**WRITING AND DRAFTING** *Priscilla Sarton*	1
Chapter 1	WRITING AND DRAFTING	3
	1.1 Introduction	3
	1.2 Drafting a legal document	3
	1.3 Writing letters	22
	1.4 Writing reports and memoranda	24
	1.5 Further reading	26
PART II	**PRACTICAL LEGAL RESEARCH** *Susan Scorey and Allun Thomas*	27
Chapter 2	INTRODUCTION TO PRACTICAL LEGAL RESEARCH	29
	2.1 The object of this Part	29
	2.2 Elements of legal research	29
	2.3 Scope of this Resource Book	30
	2.4 Library skills: objectives	31
	2.5 Types of search	32
	2.6 Updating	33
	2.7 Further reading	33
Chapter 3	CHECKING THE LAW	35
	3.1 Introduction	35
	3.2 Practitioner books	35
	3.3 *Halsbury's Laws of England*	37
Chapter 4	CITATION AND USE OF PRIMARY SOURCES	39
	4.1 Legislative materials	39
	4.2 Judicial decisions	43
Chapter 5	FINDING PRIMARY SOURCES	47
	5.1 Legislative materials	47
	5.2 Finding case-law	53
	5.3 *Current Law*	53
	5.4 Very recent developments	56
Chapter 6	EC LAW	59
	6.1 Introduction	59
	6.2 Primary legislation	60
	6.3 Secondary legislation	60
	6.4 Information on proposed legislation	64
	6.5 Case-law	65
	6.6 CELEX	66
Chapter 7	THE ELECTRONIC LAW LIBRARY	67
	7.1 Introduction to electronic materials	67
	7.2 Introduction to CD-ROMs	68
	7.3 Introduction to on-line materials	69

viii   *Skills for Lawyers*

Chapter 8	THE RESULTS OF LEGAL RESEARCH	71
	8.1 Introduction	71
	8.2 Recording research	71
	8.3 Reporting	71

PART III	**ORAL COMMUNICATION SKILLS**	**73**

Chapter 9	INTRODUCTION TO ORAL COMMUNICATION SKILLS	75
	Michael Petley	
	9.1 General	75
	9.2 Listening	75
	9.3 Questioning	76
	9.4 Non-verbal communication	77

Chapter 10	INTERVIEWING AND ADVISING *Gemma Shield*	79
	10.1 Objectives of a solicitor/client interview	79
	10.2 Common failings	79
	10.3 Two ingredients for success – skills and structure	79
	10.4 The skills	81
	10.5 Structure and management	88
	10.6 Further reading	96

Chapter 11	NEGOTIATION *Deborah Green*	97
	11.1 Introduction	97
	11.2 Aims of negotiation	97
	11.3 The ethical aspects of negotiating	98
	11.4 Negotiating styles	98
	11.5 Preparation for a negotiation	102
	11.6 Other considerations before a meeting	108
	11.7 Overview of a negotiation	110
	11.8 The opening	111
	11.9 The middle phase: discussion and bargaining	112
	11.10 The end: closing a negotiation	115
	11.11 'Dirty tricks'	115
	11.12 The forum for the negotiation	117
	11.13 Alternative dispute resolution	118
	11.14 Further reading	119

Chapter 12	ADVOCACY *John Holtam*	121
	12.1 Introduction	121
	12.2 Skills	121
	12.3 The basics	123
	12.4 Opening the case	128
	12.5 Examination-in-chief	129
	12.6 Cross-examination	133
	12.7 Re-examination	135
	12.8 Closing the case	136
	12.9 Ethical issues	137
	12.10 Criminal cases: bail and mitigation	138
	12.11 Civil cases: chambers applications	140
	12.12 Conclusion	144
	12.13 Further reading	144

INDEX		**145**

PART I

WRITING AND DRAFTING

Chapter 1

WRITING AND DRAFTING

1.1 INTRODUCTION

1.1.1 A solicitor's written skills

This chapter provides an introduction to the skills required by a solicitor when writing letters, reports and memoranda, and drafting legal documents.

1.1.2 How to approach this material

The notes which follow encourage you to think about the way in which you write and draft. You should apply these principles throughout all the subjects on the Legal Practice Course, not merely in exercises designed specifically to test writing and drafting. The principles of legal drafting will be further expanded in relation to the types of legal document relevant to individual subjects. You may find, however, that some solicitors' firms have their own style guides and precedents which they require you to follow, regardless of other recommendations.

1.2 DRAFTING A LEGAL DOCUMENT

We are considering here the drafting of a document that is intended to have legal effect. It is vital to remember that the putting of words onto your paper or your computer screen is one of the later steps in the drafting process. You must be certain of what you want your document to achieve before you look for words that will achieve it.

1.2.1 Preliminary steps

The preliminary steps are:
- taking instructions from your client;
- deciding how to put those instructions into effect;
- researching the law.

Taking instructions

To begin with, you must take instructions from your client. You need to know what your client wants to accomplish, and all the background facts.

However, you cannot rely on a client's instructions being complete. He may not think of every eventuality. For example, two clients who are setting up in partnership together and instructing you to draft the partnership agreement may not think to give you instructions as to provisions about taking holidays, or for payment of interest on

Chapter 1 contents
Introduction
Drafting a legal document
Writing letters
Writing reports and memoranda
Further reading

capital. It is part of your role as draftsperson to raise these issues, advise your client and ask for further instructions.

Equally, your client may not realise that his instructions are impossible to carry out, either practically or legally. He may instruct you to impose an obligation on a buyer of part of his land to put up a 2 metre fence along what will become the common boundary. You must realise:

- that you need further details as to what type of fence this is to be;

- that a time-limit must be imposed;

- that you need to think about compelling the neighbour not just to put up the fence but to maintain it as well;

- that a fence of that height will need planning permission and that the buyer may not be able to get the permission;

- that an obligation to erect a fence is a positive obligation, so that although your client will be able to compel the **buyer** to fulfil the obligation, there are legal difficulties in the way of enforcing the obligation against anybody who may later acquire the land.

These are all matters that you must consider and, possibly, discuss with your client and on which you might have to advise him. If you do not do this, your draft cannot be fully successful.

Deciding how to put the instructions into effect

This brings us back to the fundamental questions which underlie all legal drafting: 'What are we trying to achieve and what is the best way of achieving it?'

You must analyse your instructions. The following two questions are worth asking yourself.

(1) Am I restricting an existing right or am I granting a new one?
(2) Do I wish to impose an obligation on X, or to give him a right or a permission?

Let us tie this down to a simple example.

Suppose our client owns an outbuilding which has a small yard attached. He asks us to grant a lease of the area to X, and tells us that X is not to be allowed to park more than one car in the yard. When we come to deal with the question of parking, we must decide what it is our client wants us to do, in the light of the surrounding facts. If the lease is to be only of the outbuilding, then X will have no right to enter the yard unless the lease gives him that right. So we will carry out our instructions by including in the lease the right to park one car in the yard. If the lease is to be of the outbuilding **and** the yard, then X, as tenant, will have the power to do anything in the yard he likes. So this time, in order to carry out our instructions, we will draft a covenant by X that will restrict his right to park cars.

Suppose we are drafting such a covenant. Do you think the following covenant is suitable?

The Tenant covenants to park only one car in the Yard.

The covenant appears to impose an obligation on X to park a car. However, we do not intend to force him to park a car. We only want to ensure that he never parks more than one. So we should change the wording to:

The Tenant covenants not to park more than one car in the Yard.

This process of analysing your instructions and considering how to put them into effect is essential. A well organised, clearly written document is worse than useless if it achieves the wrong result.

Researching the law

You must know the relevant law. If you do not, it is impossible for you to judge the result of your draft.

1.2.2 Beginning to structure the document

When you have decided how to achieve your client's wishes, you can begin to plan the document. This can be done by:

- listing the points that the document must make;
- grouping the points into topics and giving each topic a heading;
- deciding in what order to deal with the topics.

For example, suppose that you are drafting an agreement for the hire of a car to a company. You might group together all the points that concern restrictions on the use of the car, for example:

- car to be used only by three named drivers;
- the company to warrant that the named drivers all hold full driving licences;
- car to be used only for specified purposes.

These points could then be put under the heading '**Use of Car**'.

Similarly, under the heading '**Deposit**' you could group such points as:

- promise by the company to pay a deposit of £500;
- provision for return of the deposit in certain circumstances;
- provision for retention of the deposit.

By doing this, you are planning the clauses in your document. You will also have to decide in what order to put the clauses.

1.2.3 Deciding on the structure of a document

A basic structure

Many documents will contain the following elements:

- commencement;
- date;
- parties;
- recitals;
- operative part;
- testimonium;
- schedules;
- execution and attestation.

COMMENCEMENT, DATE AND PARTIES

A document will normally begin with a 'commencement' which describes the nature of the document, for example 'This Agreement', 'This Conveyance'. Alternatively, the document's title can simply be printed as a heading. Deeds may also use the word 'deed' in the title, for example 'This deed of Conveyance'.

A space should be left for insertion of the date when the document is completed.

The full names and addresses of the parties should be inserted. (In the case of a company, the address of its registered office should be inserted.) For example:

SERVICE AGREEMENT

DATE:

PARTIES: (1) **Weyford Products Limited whose registered office is at 32 Bridge House, Wharf Road, Milton, Berefordshire.**

(2) **Joan Alice Bennet of 8 High Street, Milton, Berefordshire.**

A long and complicated document can benefit from an index or table of clauses (preferably at the front).

RECITALS

Recitals clauses are not essential and you should consider carefully whether or not to include them. You can use them to set out the background facts to the document and so make it more self-explanatory. For example, in a conveyance of land by a personal representative the date of the deceased's death and the date on which a grant of representation was obtained could be recited.

Recitals are also sometimes used to introduce and summarise the contents of the operative part of the document but, except in complicated documents, this is generally not necessary and increases the risk of introducing ambiguities.

OPERATIVE PART

The operative part of a document is the part which creates the legal rights and obligations.

The contents of the operative part of a document depend on the nature of the document. For example, a commercial agreement will generally contain:

- conditions precedent (setting out conditions which have to be satisfied before the agreement comes into force);
- agreements (setting out the rights and obligations of the parties);
- representations and warranties (ie statements about factual and legal matters which one of the parties requires to be made to him in a legally binding way);
- 'boiler-plate' clauses (ie standard clauses inserted into all agreements of such a type and dealing with, for example, the service of notices under the agreement, or the jurisdiction for action where the agreement has an international element).

TESTIMONIUM

A testimonium clause is not essential but, if used, it introduces the signatures of the parties and may describe a particular method of executing where, for example, a company is using its seal as part of its execution, or an attorney is signing on behalf of a party.

SCHEDULES

Use schedules where appropriate to avoid breaking the continuity of a document with too much detail. The operative part of the document then refers to the schedule, and the schedule contains the detail. For example:

TENANT'S COVENANTS

The Tenant covenants with the Landlord to observe and perform the covenants set out in Schedule 1.

SCHEDULE 1

1. To pay the rent ... etc.

Note that the obligation or right is created in the operative part of the document. Only the detail of the obligation or right is put in the schedule.

EXECUTION AND ATTESTATION

A document will end with an execution clause. This will refer to the signatures of the parties and any other formalities necessary to give the document legal effect. The wording of this clause will vary depending on the nature of the party executing, whether the document is executed as a deed, and whether the party's signature is witnessed ('attested').

For a document executed by an individual and not intended to take effect as a deed, the clause could read:

Signed by ALAN JONES)	**(Alan Jones**
in the presence of:)	**signs here)**
(Witness signs here)	

If the document is intended to take effect as a deed the clause could read:

Executed as a deed)	**(Alan Jones**
by ALAN JONES)	**signs here)**
in the presence of:)	
(Witness signs here)	

Order of clauses in the operative part

It is difficult to lay down rules as to the order of clauses. It will vary according to the nature of the document, but is often a matter of common sense and logic.

CHRONOLOGICAL ORDER

One possibility is to list topics in chronological order. This is often particularly suitable for a document that deals with one simple transaction.

Imagine a contract for the hire of a car. The order of topics could be:

- parties;
- definitions;
- agreement by Owner to hire out car to Hirer on the terms set out in the agreement;
- payment;
- insurance;
- promises by Owner as to the state of the car at the start of the hire;
- duration of hire;
- what the car can be used for;
- who may drive;
- Hirer's promises as to the return of the car;
- remedies for breach of the agreement.

For a contract such as this, a chronological structure will produce a simpler and less repetitious document than if you try to divide topics into Owner's Obligations and Hirer's Obligations.

CATEGORICAL ORDER

A categorical structure sets out the duties and responsibilities in categories. An example of this is a lease.

The structure of a typical lease is:

- parties;
- definitions;
- the grant of the term by Landlord to Tenant;
- Tenant's covenants;
- Landlord's covenants;
- provisos, for example the Landlord's power to forfeit the lease.

Here, the division into landlord's obligations and tenant's obligations is essential. The obligations have to be performed throughout the entire term of the lease. There is no chronological order to them.

ORDER OF IMPORTANCE

This could be the order used in a simple contract, where the obligations are not to be carried out in any chronological order. An example could be an agreement between employer and employee on severance of employment.

A document may use a combination of these orders. A contract with a firm of furniture removers could list the firm's obligations in chronological order, for example:

- to pack the contents of the house;
- to transport to storage;

- to store;
- to transport to new house;
- to unpack;

and then list the owner's obligations.

In a lease, all the tenant's covenants will be put together, but will appear in order of importance.

1.2.4 Checking the draft

When you have finished the draft, check it carefully. To do this you must check:

- that it is carrying out your clients instructions, and that it is carrying out **all** of them. If you began by listing all the points that the document would have to cover, take the list and check off each item against the relevant clause;
- that the meaning of each sentence is unambiguous;
- the numbering of clauses;
- all cross-references in the document to other clauses or to schedules. References can easily become inaccurate if clauses are added to or deleted from the original draft;
- the headings to your clauses. Does the heading correctly represent the contents of the clause?
- the names of the parties;
- all figures and dates;
- spelling and grammar. Do not rely entirely on the 'spell check' on your computer. It will not reveal a mistake such as using 'principle' for 'principal'.

If possible, leave some time before making your final check. A fresh eye might spot mistakes previously overlooked.

1.2.5 Further points on drafting

Now that we have considered general principles, we shall look at particular points in more detail.

Definitions

USE OF DEFINITIONS

A definition can do two things.

It can create a '**tag**' or '**nickname**'. This avoids repetition of names or lengthy phrases. This use is seen in the description of the parties to a document. For example:

> **This agreement is made between**
>
> **(1) Kingdom Finance Plc [the Company]**
>
> **(2) Edward Burns [the Borrower]**

In the rest of the document it is only necessary to refer to the Company and the Borrower.

Another example is:

In this agreement

1. 'the Period of Hire' means from 9am on 1 November 2000 until noon on 23 November 2000.

Later clauses can then say things such as:

if the Hirer does not return the Car at or before the end of the Period of Hire ...

It can create a private dictionary for the document by giving a word something other than its ordinary meaning, or by giving a word an unusually extended or restricted meaning.

For example:

In this agreement

'Boat' includes a sailboard

Note that it is usual to give the definition a capital letter, and use it with the capital letter throughout the document. This alerts anybody reading it to the fact that a particular word or expression has been given a particular meaning by the document.

WHERE TO PUT THE DEFINITIONS

Definitions that are to apply throughout the document should be put in alphabetical order in a definitions clause at the start of the operative part of the document.

DEFINITIONS

In this Agreement

(1) 'Arbitration' means ...

(2) 'Balance Sheet' means ... etc

If a definition will be used only in one part of a document or in one clause, you can put the definition at the start of the relevant part or clause.

4.1 In this clause, 'Promotional Material' means ...

4.2 The Landowner must ensure that all Promotional Material is ...

In a simple document, a 'tag' may be given to a name or phrase the first time that it is used, and the tag may then be used throughout the rest of the document. For example, in a contract for the sale of land, a clause may say:

The Seller, for the benefit of his adjoining property, 10 Smith Avenue, Morton, N. Yorks ('the Retained Land') reserves a right of way on foot ...

Later clauses can then refer to the Retained Land.

This method should be used only for simple short documents. In a long document, it will be a waste of time to have to search through the clauses to find the one in which the tag was first bestowed.

SOME GROUND RULES FOR USING DEFINITIONS

1. Do not define a term if you are going to use the term in its ordinary dictionary meaning.

For example, suppose that a person hiring a room is to be given a right to bring tables into it. If the owner of the room does not care what sort of the tables they are, do not define the word 'table'.

However, if for some reason, only tables of a certain size are to be allowed, you could deal with this by a definition.

In this agreement, 'Table' means a table that is no longer than two metres, and no wider than one metre.

In such a simple example as this, it might be better not to use a definition but to restrict the right. In other words, instead of defining table, and later saying 'the Hirer may bring six Tables into the room', you could say:

The Hirer may bring six tables into the room but no table may be longer than two metres or wider than one metre.

It depends on whether or not you need a definition for other clauses.

2. A definition should only define. It should not be used to create a substantive right or obligation. The right or obligation should be created in the clause that uses the definition.

3. If you have a definition, do not forget to use it when you are drafting the rest of the document.

4. Whenever you use a defined term in a clause, check back to the definition. Does the definition make sense in this clause?

5. In a definition, do not define by reference to other undefined terms. For example,

   In this Agreement

   'Property' includes preliminary and reserved options.

   This definition may be meaningless without a definition of preliminary and reserved options.

Structuring a clause

STRUCTURING CLAUSES AND SUBCLAUSES WITHIN THE OPERATIVE PART

1. Use a separate clause for each separate matter.

2. Use sub-paragraphing to avoid long, cumbersome clauses and provisos.

   Consider:

   1. The Licensee shall purchase exclusively from the Grantor all materials used in making the Invention PROVIDED that the Licensee shall be entitled to relieve itself of its liability to observe this obligation upon giving the Grantor three months' notice in writing.

   Compare:

   1. Subject to Clause 2, the Licensee shall purchase exclusively from the Grantor all materials used in making the Invention.

   2. The Licensee may end the obligation contained in Clause 1 by giving the Grantor three months' notice in writing.

3. Number each clause and sub-clause.

4. Give each clause or group of clauses a heading that correctly defines the subject matter of the clauses, eg:

Tenant's Covenants

STRUCTURING A CLAUSE ACCORDING TO COODE

Consider:

The Company shall reimburse the Replacement Value provided that the value of the claim does not exceed £1,000 and the Policyholder notifies the loss within 7 days from (but excluding) the date of its occurrence PROVIDED ALWAYS THAT the above shall not apply to claims made under Clause 10 of this Policy.

This clause starts with a statement of a legal obligation which at first sight appears absolute. The conditions and exceptions attaching to the obligation are not stated until afterwards, so that it is necessary to reconsider the obligation in the light of them. This kind of clause construction is very common in legal drafting but it is not the most logical way to structure a clause and it makes it more difficult to understand.

In 1843, George Coode wrote a treatise on 'Legislative Expression'; or, 'The Language of The Written Law'. His general principle is that a clause should be structured in the following order:

- circumstances/exceptions (ie circumstances where the right or obligation does or does not exist);

- conditions (ie conditions on which the right or obligation depends);

- obligation or right (ie who **must** do what or who **may** do what).

Words suitable for introducing an exception are 'except where ...'

Words suitable for introducing circumstances are 'where ...' 'if ... then' or 'when ...' or 'on ...'.

Words suitable for introducing conditions are 'if ...' or 'provided that ...'.

These are two examples of Coode in legislation.

Section 2(1) of the Land Registration and Land Charges Act 1971:

'**If** any question arises as to whether a person is entitled to an indemnity under any provision of the Land Registration Act 1925 [*circumstance*] [...] **he** [*person*] **may apply** to the court to have that question determined [*the right*].'

Section 23(1) of the Matrimonial Causes Act 1973:

'**On** granting a decree of divorce ... [*circumstance*] **the court** [*person*] **may make** any one or more of the following orders ... [*right*].'

This is an example of Coode in a document.

15 Compensation on termination of contract

Except where otherwise provided [*exception*], if before 1 December 2001 this contract is terminated by the Buyer, [*circumstance*] then provided the Seller is not in breach of any of his obligations under this contract [*condition*] the Buyer shall pay the Seller the sum of £5000 [*obligation*].

The rule produces a logical, and to lawyers, a familiar structure, but it does not have invariably to be followed.

Imagine that an owner of land has employed consultants to design and build an amusement park. The consultants want to control the use of their name in any advertising material issued by the landowner. Their name is to be used only if certain conditions are met.

If the clause were drafted using Coode's rule, it would read:

Only where

(a) the Landowner has given the Consultants advance details of any advertising material it plans to use; and

(b) the Consultants have given their express written approval; and

(c) the Consultants have not ended this Agreement under sub-clause 11(1)

may the Landowner use the Consultant's name in advertising material.

The clause could make the point in a more natural and in a stronger manner if Coode were ignored and the clause were drafted to read:

The Landowner may only use the Consultants' name in advertising material where:

(a) the Landowner has given the Consultants advance details of any advertising materials it plans to use; and

(b) the Consultants have given their express written approval; and

(c) the Consultants have not ended this Agreement under sub-clause 11(1).

Layout and presentation of the document

PARAGRAPHS

Using paragraphs makes prose more readable and helps to avoid cumbersome clauses and sub-clauses.

TABULATION

Tabulation may help to avoid ambiguity.

Consider the sentence:

Any trainee solicitor is entitled to paid leave to attend a conference, lecture, or seminar *provided by The Law Society*.

How much of the sentence is the phrase in italics intended to qualify? Does it apply only to 'seminar', or to 'conference' and 'lecture' as well?

Compare:

Any trainee solicitor is entitled to paid leave to attend:

(a) a conference; or

(b) a lecture; or

(c) a seminar,

provided by The Law Society.

Care should be taken, however, not to indent the final phrase 'provided by The Law Society' to the same margin as 'a seminar' or the ambiguity would remain.

NUMBERING

Where a series of points is being made, numbering may improve clarity and aid later cross-referencing.

Examples of numbering systems:

> 4.5.1 The system adopted in this Resource Book and known as the decimal system.
>
> 4(5)(a)(i) A system based on the legislative approach and known as the alpha-numeric system.
>
> 4.5(a)(i) A combination system using elements of both decimal and alpha-numeric systems.

1.2.6 Use of precedents

A precedent is a good servant and a bad master. Do not start drafting from a precedent until you have analysed your client's instructions and decided what you want to achieve. If you turn to a precedent immediately, you will find that it controls you instead of being a helpful tool.

Using a precedent has the following benefits:

- the precedent might suggest a suitable structure for your document;
- it might suggest provisions that you have not thought of and that will benefit your client;
- it might suggest suitable wording;
- the introductory notes and footnotes might alert you to legal problems that you had not thought of.

It has the following perils:

- the precedent might suggest an unsuitable structure. In particular, it might tempt you into a long and complex document, when a simple one is all that is needed;
- it might tempt you to include clauses that are irrelevant, or worse, are to the disadvantage of your client;
- it might suggest inappropriate or archaic wording;
- the notes on law will lead you astray if the law has changed since the date the precedent was published.

Guidelines on the use of precedents

- Always decide what you want your document to do before you consider the precedents.
- Accept the fact there may be no precedent that exactly covers your situation.
- Adapt the precedent to your transaction; not your transaction to the precedent.
- Use modern precedents. Even modern precedents may have to be altered if the law has recently changed.

- Be careful if you bring a clause from a precedent into your draft document. The clause may have to be altered to follow the definitions in your draft, or to match its style or language. Sometimes, the clause which you bring in makes no sense without a definition in its parent document. Remember to alter the clause, or to bring in the definition as well.

- Do not copy words from a precedent unless you are sure of their legal effect.

- Do not change words in a precedent unless you are sure that the change will not have an unexpected legal effect. This is particularly true of precedents for wills.

- Be wary of using as a precedent a document which was drafted by someone else for some other transaction. The fact that a document has been used in another transaction does not necessarily make it a good precedent. Also, the document might have been slanted in favour of the party by whose solicitor it was drafted.

1.2.7 Language

Note: the following advice is applicable not only to the drafting of documents, but applies also to the writing of letters, reports and memoranda.

The following are sensible rules:

- use simple and direct language;
- keep sentences and paragraphs short;
- think before you use the passive;
- avoid ambiguity;
- be careful how you use 'shall' and 'will'.

Simple and direct language

'PADDING'

Try to avoid the use of unnecessary phrases which lengthen the sentence while adding nothing to its meaning. For example:

- 'until such time as';
- 'in this instance';
- 'the fact that';
- 'of course'.

TOO MANY ADJECTIVES?

Consider whether the noun requires an adjective at all. In the following examples, the adjective adds nothing to the noun:

- 'true facts';
- 'terrible disaster';
- 'unfilled vacancy'.

Try to avoid a string of similar adjectives which do not make the meaning more precise. For example:

- 'grave and fatal error';
- 'careful and detailed consideration'.

COMPOUND PREPOSITIONS

Try to avoid using a phrase where a single preposition will do. For example:

- 'in accordance with' (by, under);
- 'by reason of' (by, through);
- 'with reference to' (about);
- 'in order to' (to).

NOUNS DERIVED FROM VERBS

Could you use the verb itself rather than a noun derived from it? (This often creates a more immediate effect.)

- 'make an admission' (admit);
- 'give consideration to' (consider);
- 'effect a termination' (terminate or end);

JARGON

Try to avoid jargon unless you are sure the recipient will be familiar with it. For example:

- 'mortgage-sourcing information';
- 'clothing-optional beaches'.

'LEGALESE'

If possible, avoid archaic words and phrases such as:

- 'herewith';
- 'herein';
- 'hereinbefore';
- 'hereby';
- 'crave leave';
- 'the said ...'.

LEGAL TERMS

Legal terms should be translated for lay clients. For example:

- 'joint tenancy';
- 'decree nisi'.

Short sentences and paragraphs

USE SHORT SENTENCES

In long sentences the verb, subject and object may be separated by too many sub-clauses. This places a strain on the reader's memory and understanding. Consider, for example:

> **The evidence, including evidence from independent surveys as well as that gathered personally by the writers of this report and the results of investigations formally commissioned by this department, suggests that the public, while acknowledging an overall increase in the actual level of**

government spending on health, by which is meant on health care both at the doctor–patient level and in hospitals, still views the problems and defects in the National Health Service and in particular in National Health hospitals as the result of a general lack of funding.

The sub-clauses break up the main thought of the paragraph so that it is difficult to follow. The paragraph would be better rewritten in separate sentences with the main thought first, even though this may increase its length. Brackets can be used for subsidiary points where appropriate. For example:

The evidence suggests that the public still views the problems and defects in the National Health Service and in particular in National Health hospitals as the result of a general lack of funding. This is so even though it acknowledges an overall increase in the actual level of government spending on health care both at the doctor–patient level and in hospitals. (Evidence on this issue includes evidence from independent surveys, that gathered personally by the writers of this report and the results of investigations formally commissioned by this department.)

Verbs in the passive

ACTIVE AND PASSIVE VOICE

In a sentence where the verb is in the active voice, the subject of the sentence acts upon the object of the sentence. Where the verb is in the passive voice, the object of the sentence is acted upon by the subject. Compare:

The defendant struck the plaintiff (active voice).

The plaintiff was struck by the defendant (passive voice).

PROBLEMS WITH THE PASSIVE

Over-use of the passive voice lengthens a sentence and can make it sound weak. In the worst cases, it obscures meaning. For example:

It is hoped that resources will be relocated so that changes may be made in the methods by which the system is administered.

Where the verb is in the passive you may accidentally omit the phrase which indicates who or what is doing the acting. For example:

The plaintiff was struck.

In a legal context, the effect of this omission may be important. For example:

Notice will be served. By whom?

SOME USES FOR THE PASSIVE

The passive can sound more objective and detached and therefore more appropriate in certain legal contexts. For example:

The allegations are denied

sounds better than:

Our client denies the allegations, which introduces a personal note.

It is correct to use the passive where the subject of the legal action is irrelevant. For example:

The common seal of X Co was affixed.... It does not matter who affixed it.

The passive can also be used in a legal context to cover the possibility of action by a number of different persons, some of whom are unknown. For example:

If the goods are damaged we will refund the cost. This could cover damage by the supplier, the carrier, or any third party.

Ambiguity

TAKE CARE WITH WORD ORDER

Words or phrases in the wrong place may create ambiguity.

Consider the sentence:

We undertake to repair or replace goods shown to be defective *within six months of the date of purchase.*

It is not clear whether the phrase in italics governs the repair/replacement or the notification of defect. It could be rewritten as:

Where, within six months of the date of purchase, goods are shown to be defective, we will repair or replace them (assuming this was the intended meaning).

DO YOU MEAN 'AND' OR 'OR'?

Consider:

The Seller may serve notice of termination, recover goods already delivered and retain all instalments already paid.

The use of 'and' in this sentence suggests that the list is conjunctive, ie that the seller may do all of the things in it. But can he choose to do only some of them?

Compare:

The Seller may serve notice of termination, recover goods already delivered or retain all instalments already paid.

The use of 'or' here suggests that the list is disjunctive, ie that the seller may do only one of the things in the list. But it could also mean that he may *both* serve notice *and* either recover goods or retain instalments.

To avoid such ambiguity, consider (depending on the meaning required) using phrases such as:

The Seller may do all or any of the following:

or

The Seller may exercise one only of the following rights:

THE 'UNDISTRIBUTED MIDDLE'

Take care with provisions 'before/after' a particular date or 'over/under' a particular weight or measure.

Consider the following examples:

> **Where the company delivers the goods before 1 January ... / Where the company delivers the goods after 1 January ...**

What happens if it delivers them *on* 1 January?

> **Goods over 40lb must be sent by rail ... / Goods under 40lb may be sent by air**

What about goods weighing *exactly* 40lb?

EXPRESSIONS OF TIME

Take care to avoid ambiguity.

Consider:

> **The Buyer must pay a deposit within 7 days of today's date.**

Does the 7 days include or exclude today?

For legal and practical reasons, avoid expressing periods of time in the following ways:

- from [a date];
- by [a date];
- within [so many days of] or from [a date];
- until [a date].

It is safer to be clear by using one of the following:

- from but excluding/not including;
- from and including;
- on or after;
- on or before;
- within a period of 7 days commencing with;
- until but excluding/not including;
- until and including.

ARE YOU CREATING AN OBLIGATION OR A DISCRETION?

An obligation is created by the phrase:

> **The Customer shall pay a deposit on signing this Agreement.**

A discretion is created by the phrase:

> **The Company may retain the deposit if the Customer does not collect the goods on or before 30 June.**

Take care when using 'shall'. It is grammatically correct to use it in the third person to indicate an obligation ('the Tenant shall pay the Rent') but it can also be used in the first person to indicate simple future ('I shall go to London'). Alternatively, you could use 'must' to create an obligation.

AVOID WORDS OF SIMILAR SOUND OR APPEARANCE

Words of similar sound or appearance can be accidentally transposed by a typist and may also confuse a lay client. For example:

Avoid	*Use instead*
'mortgagor/mortgagee'	'lender/borrower'
'lessor/lessee'	'landlord/tenant'

AMBIGUOUS PRONOUNS

Consider:

> **Where the Supplier fails to deliver the Goods to the Customer in accordance with Clause 9 or the Goods delivered do not correspond with the sample he may terminate this Agreement.**

Who may terminate the agreement?

Where it is not clear to which noun a pronoun refers, the noun should be repeated.

THE EJUSDEM GENERIS RULE

Consider:

> **In consequence of war, disturbance or any other cause.**

Unless a contrary intention appears, 'any other cause' will be construed as meaning only causes in the same category as those previously listed.

To avoid ambiguity, add (as appropriate):

> **whether of the same kind as [the causes] previously listed or not** or
>
> **or any other [cause] provided it is of the same kind as the [causes] previously listed.**

BLANKS

Try to minimise the number of blanks for completion to reduce the risk that they are left uncompleted.

Shall/will

In the first person, 'shall' simply looks to the future. In the second and third person, 'will' looks to the future.

> **I shall interview the client tomorrow. I hope that you will sit in. Afterwards, we shall discuss the drafting.**

In the first person, 'will' expresses determination. In the second or third person, 'shall' expresses determination or obligation.

> **I will make you do this.**
>
> **The Buyer shall pay £500 on the 1 December.**

This means that you create problems if your document says 'the Buyer will pay ...' Is this what he intends to do or is it what he is obligated to do?

Many documents use expressions such as 'If the Company shall breach this term ...'. The clause is looking to the future but is using 'shall' incorrectly. It could be redrafted to say 'In the event of the company breaking ...'. It is simpler to say 'If the Company breaks ...'.

1.2.8 Practical and ethical considerations when drafting

Good practice when submitting a draft

Out of courtesy, you should always supply to the other side an additional copy of any draft sent for approval.

Use a layout which helps the other side to read and amend the draft; for example, use wide margins and double spacing.

Good practice when amending the other side's draft

Amend a draft by hand so that the amendments are clear. Do not have the draft retyped or the amendments will become difficult for the other side to identify.

Do not erase another firm's word processor identification markings. It will be important for them to identify the disk quickly.

If you receive a draft which is substantially acceptable but in a style of drafting which you do not favour, it is tactless to redraft it in a different style and will not improve relations with that firm. The most you can do is to correct any errors and hope that any draft you send them in the future may influence them to change their style!

Ethical considerations when negotiating a draft

Two rules of professional conduct are relevant.

(1) A solicitor must not act, whether in his professional capacity or otherwise, towards anyone in a way which is fraudulent, deceitful or otherwise contrary to his position as a solicitor, nor must he use his position as a solicitor to take unfair advantage either for himself or another person.
(2) A solicitor must act towards other solicitors with complete frankness and good faith consistent with the overriding duty to his client.

Breach of these rules renders the solicitor liable to disciplinary action.

Do not attempt to mislead the other side by concealing amendments you have made to their draft, for example by writing a covering letter which draws attention to some amendments and not to others. Any deliberate attempt to mislead could be criminally fraudulent as well as amounting to professional misconduct.

Do not attempt to take advantage of a mistake made by the other side. Point it out to them. They may otherwise be able to claim rectification of the document to incorporate an omitted provision or allege that the agreement is a nullity, so enabling them to resist specific performance.

1.3 WRITING LETTERS

1.3.1 Who is the addressee?

Consider the needs of the reader and try to adapt your style accordingly.

The lay client

Take care to avoid jargon and legalese when writing to a lay client. Explain all unfamiliar terms, but try not to make the tone patronising. How familiar is the client with the subject?

The business client

The business client will generally be familiar with solicitors' letters, so avoid verbosity and get to the point quickly.

Other professionals

Other professionals may need some legal terms translated.

Other solicitors

What kind of matter are you dealing with? Are you writing from a position of strength or weakness? Do you want to adopt a conciliatory or non-conciliatory stance? Consider which is more likely to persuade the addressee. Remember that the other solicitor may send a copy of your letter to his client.

1.3.2 'Ghosting'

You may be asked to write letters to be signed in a partner's own name. Read the file and consider the partner's style. Check how well the partner knows the addressee; for example, if you are writing to a client, is the partner on first-name terms with him?

1.3.3 Starting and ending the letter

Generally

Letters beginning 'Dear Sirs/Sir/Madam' all end 'Yours faithfully'.

A letter addressed to a person by surname, for example 'Dear Mr Smith', ends with 'Yours sincerely'.

A letter beginning 'Dear John' may end with 'Yours sincerely' or 'Yours' (either of which could be prefixed by a phrase such as 'Kind regards' or 'Best wishes').

Female addressees

Where possible, try to find out a woman's preference in advance, for example 'Miss', 'Mrs', or 'Ms'. As an alternative, some writers use 'Dear Jane Smith' if 'Dear Madam' would be too formal and 'Dear Jane' too informal.

1.3.4 Content

Consider overall structure

An initial heading identifying the matter is conventional. For example:

Jones to Smith
Sale of 25 Acacia Avenue, Bristol

A complex letter will be easier to understand (and reply to) if you give each paragraph a number and a heading.

Form and style

If you are writing in the firm's name (eg a formal letter to the other side), write in the first person plural ('we') and be consistent.

Acknowledge the addressee's last communication.

If it is your first letter to the addressee, explain your involvement.

State the purpose of the letter.

Carry out that purpose using:

- logical sequence;
- separate paragraphs;
- short sentences;
- active voice.

Write in a restrained tone. Avoid over-emphasis (eg unnecessary adverbs – 'totally unhappy', 'completely inaccurate'). Rarely use exclamation marks. Do not express surprise, amazement, outrage, etc.

Avoid jokes and witticisms.

1.3.5 Some practical points

Second thoughts and improvements

Try to be detached about your letter. How will it appear through another's eyes?

How would it sound if read out in open court in the future?

Try not to write a letter in a temper or in an emotional state. If you do, do not post it until you have had a chance to re-read it or a colleague has reviewed it.

Consider giving a deadline for a reply (eg if the matter is urgent or if the letter might be unwelcome).

If you have asked a client to do something, are your instructions clear?

Check the grammar and spelling.

Final checks

Check that the letter:

- carries the correct references (ie yours and those of the other side);
- is dated;
- is signed;
- is accompanied by the right enclosures;
- is put into the right envelope, and is properly addressed.

1.4 WRITING REPORTS AND MEMORANDA

1.4.1 Reports

Purpose

Reports usually cover a specific subject and serve a particular purpose. In the office you may have to write a report on some legal research or fact-finding you were asked to undertake.

Is your research complete?

Consider whether you have all the necessary information and identify any gaps.

Edit your material

Consider how much information should go into the report. Brevity increases the likelihood of the report being read, but too little information may not adequately support your conclusions.

Planning your report

Plan the text of your report carefully to produce a logical argument.

Consider what will be the most useful structure for the reader. For example, if you were asked to answer specific questions could you use these to head paragraphs of your report?

Consider including:

- a contents page or index;
- an introduction explaining why the report was commissioned;
- a brief summary of the report before the main text for quick reference;
- diagrams (if relevant);
- case or statute references (if relevant);
- a bibliography;
- appendices;
- acknowledgments of sources of information.

Style

For whom are you writing? Adapt your style appropriately.

Consider whether you should paraphrase or explain your source material, or whether you can reproduce it word for word.

Layout and presentation

Make sure the report is well set out, with clear headings and numbered paragraphs and sub-paragraphs if appropriate.

Is it to be used as a discussion document? If so, consider having it typed in double spacing with wide margins to leave room for others to write notes.

Final checks

Have the report typed in draft form first. Read it through carefully, amending and rewriting where necessary.

Check that you have:

- done what you were asked to do;
- identified any relevant options;
- reached a conclusion.

1.4.2 Memoranda

Types of memoranda

Solicitors generally have to write two types of memoranda:

- attendance notes (as a record of their meetings or telephone calls with clients, other solicitors, etc);
- internal memoranda (as a quick way of communicating with others in the firm).

Attendance notes

Attendance notes are put on a file as a record of an oral discussion, transaction or agreement and must be clear and accurate in case of any later dispute.

They are essential for anyone who takes over a file and was not present for the meeting, telephone call, etc.

They may also be needed when a client's bill is prepared as part of the record of chargeable time spent on the matter.

Write or dictate your attendance note as soon as possible after the event it records so as to avoid forgetting essential detail.

Always try to take contemporaneous notes – in a simple case you can put them straight on the file. For more complicated matters, you can use your notes to compile your attendance note, but do not destroy them; they are important additional evidence in any dispute.

An attendance note should normally contain the following:

- the client's name;
- the subject matter;
- your reference;
- the date;
- the place (of any meeting);
- the people present (at a meeting);
- the starting and finishing times (of the meeting or phone call);
- a summary of what was discussed or agreed;
- any follow-up action to be taken by you or others.

If your attendance note records an important decision or agreement, always confirm it by letter to avoid misunderstandings.

Internal memoranda

Keep internal memoranda brief and business-like, but take care with the tone. If a memo sounds curt, you may cause offence to the recipient.

The format required is generally as follows:

MEMORANDUM

From:

To:

Fee earner's reference:

Date:

Client's name:

Client's matter:

File number:

Most firms use printed forms on which these headings already appear.

1.5 FURTHER READING

Melville *Draftsman's Handbook* (Longman, 1991)
Robinson *Drafting* (Butterworth, 1980)
Berg *Drafting Commercial Agreements* (Butterworth, 1991)
Piesse and Aitken *The Elements of Drafting* (Law Book Company, 1991)
Gowers *The Complete Plain Words* (Penguin, 1987)
Fowlers *Modern English Usage* (Oxford University Press, 1983)
Adler *Clarity for Lawyers* (The Law Society, 1990)
National Consumer Council *Plain English for Lawyers* (1990)

PART II

PRACTICAL LEGAL RESEARCH

Chapter 2

INTRODUCTION TO PRACTICAL LEGAL RESEARCH

2.1 THE OBJECT OF THIS PART

The legal research Part of this Resource Book takes as its focus the inevitable moment, which will probably arise within one month of your arrival at your firm, when your principal asks you to check a point of law. The academic stage of legal education will have introduced you to legal research and the use of a law library but now, for the first time, you will be handling a problem which concerns a real client, and which tests your own competence as a practising lawyer.

In relation to legal research, this book aims to build on existing academic skills and to offer an introduction to research in practice. The most obvious difference between academic and practical research derives from the aim of the research. Most academic research will be directed to achieving a general understanding of one subject or topic. Practical research benefits from such an understanding, but it is usually more limited. Its aim is to find a solution to a specific problem of a particular client. This book focuses on practical research.

At the highest level, practical research is complex. For example, advising a client on the correct structure for a company takeover will involve the analysis of a considerable amount of factual information, familiarity with a range of areas of law, and sensitivity to the practical implications of each possible course of action. It is reasonable to assume, however, that you will not be required to begin at this level. You can expect to start by researching under supervision, in a defined area of practice, with tasks which do not stretch your capacity unduly. This Resource Book follows these assumptions. It does not offer a model of legal research which will last for life. Instead, it offers you the opportunity to adapt your academic skills to the requirements of practice before deploying them in the real world.

2.2 ELEMENTS OF LEGAL RESEARCH

Practical legal research aims at solving a specific problem for a particular client. It can be analysed as involving four separate elements.

2.2.1 Assembling the facts

Legal research cannot begin until the facts of the case have been assembled and understood. This will involve taking full instructions from a client and is dependent on the separate skill of interviewing. It is also dependent on legal analysis which will determine those facts of the case which are material. Legal analysis may require investigation of some specific facts. For example, if the client is seeking a divorce, he will be asked questions linked to establishing grounds for the divorce. In addition, extensive factual research may be required, for instance in personal injury litigation

Chapter 2 contents
The object of this Part
Elements of legal research
Scope of this Resource Book
Library skills: objectives
Types of search
Updating
Further reading

where it may take time to determine the extent and nature of the injury. In any event, where evidence is doubtful, the factual context of the research will be uncertain, and it may be necessary to base the research on a range of possible factual situations.

2.2.2 Legal analysis

Legal analysis is a core skill of a lawyer. For a solicitor, it is the process by which the client's rights are defined by reference to legal authority and principle. The techniques of analysis vary with the subject-matter. The analytical skills required in company law are quite different from those required in criminal litigation. Training in legal method may form part of an introduction to the academic stage of legal education, but after that the student becomes a lawyer by exploring the concepts of separate divisions of the law, step by step. This has implications for the objectives and structure of the legal research section of this book, which are explained below (see **2.3**).

2.2.3 Library skills

After preliminary legal analysis of a problem, the next stage usually involves use of the law library, in two possible ways.

(1) It may be necessary to check the law to confirm or extend the preliminary analysis. This will usually involve use of practitioner texts.
(2) It may be necessary to trace the primary sources for a point of law in order to provide an authority which could be cited in court. This may involve updating, ie checking that the authority has not been superseded.

Clearly, these exercises may show that the preliminary analysis was wrong, in which case the process must be repeated.

2.2.4 Applying the results

The last stage of the research process is its application to the client's problem. Advice to the client is not, of itself, one of the elements of research, but clearly the product of research must be formulated in such a way that it can form the basis of advice. It must be tailored to the needs of the client. Where you are not the adviser, for example where you carry out research for your principal, it will be necessary to provide a clear report which can form the basis of the advice given to the client.

2.3 SCOPE OF THIS RESOURCE BOOK

From the above, it should be apparent that there are difficulties in developing legal research as an independent skill. Any model for performance of the skill might be too abstract to be useful, because the core element of legal analysis is best developed in the context of particular areas of the law.

This Resource Book assumes that problem-solving as a whole is best dealt with in the context of particular subjects, but aims to provide an introduction to cover the elements which can be isolated from their context. Library skills can sensibly be dealt with in this way, if two assumptions are made. The first is that you will not have full responsibility, initially, for handling the matter researched. Instead, your principal will take responsibility for assembling the facts, and preliminary legal analysis. Your responsibility is assumed to be limited to checking the law, tracing primary sources, and reporting the results. The second assumption is that you should concentrate, initially, on general sources, rather than those which concern only a particular branch of the law, for example becoming familiar with use of *Current Law* before looking at *Simon's Tax Intelligence*.

2.4 LIBRARY SKILLS: OBJECTIVES

Library skills involve the ability to find and report the relevant material in the quickest possible time. There is no mechanical formula which will enable you to do this, but the following general points should be borne in mind.

Organising the research

Before starting, formulate a research plan. Analyse the problem. Does it involve a single issue, or a number of issues? Will different research materials be relevant to different parts of the problem? Which sources are most likely to provide an answer? Will an answer from a practitioner textbook be adequate, or is it necessary to look at primary sources? How likely is it that there have been recent changes in the law? What are the likely subject headings under which the problem might be classified? If you consider these questions first, you will be able to plan your research more effectively.

Identifying the correct sources

The ability to identify the correct sources depends on thorough familiarity with the sources available, and the following sections of the Resource Book deal with this. A common procedure will be to begin by looking at a commentary on the law, a textbook, or a general work such as *Halsbury's Laws of England*. This should direct you to a primary source, such as case-law, statute, or delegated legislation. These primary sources are authoritative, and should be checked carefully. Once you have found the primary source, you should 'update' as a matter of routine to check that the authority remains effective. Textbooks can be wrong.

Recording the research

Record the sources used and the information found. It may be that the relevance of material is realised only at the end of the research. If a record has been kept, it is possible to check back quickly without duplication of effort.

Extracting the key points

Your principal will not thank you if you report your research by producing armfuls of law reports and statutes. A written report should be produced which extracts the relevant information from the source material. The report should be a summary of material extracted as the research proceeds. This will involve the essential academic skills of interpretation of statutes and case analysis.

Reporting the results clearly

The final report of the research must be intelligible to your principal and capable of forming the basis for advice. The ability to draft a report depends on your written communication skills (see Chapter 1). However, this legal research section ends with some specific points on the form of a simple research report (see Chapter 8).

2.5 TYPES OF SEARCH

Most sources, whether commentaries on the law or collections of primary sources, will offer a choice of approach. There will usually be a subject index, and an index of primary sources referred to or reproduced in the text. Both are useful, but in different ways, and at different stages.

2.5.1 Subject index searches

A subject index should be used when you do not know of any relevant primary source. You will have used indexes in textbooks to locate general explanations of areas of law. They can also be used as a quick way of finding correct citations of relevant primary sources which will often be referred to in the text, or in footnotes. In a collection of primary sources, such as *Halsbury's Statutes*, use of a subject index may lead straight to the relevant primary source.

Using a subject index as a means of legal research is a particular skill. Look at any subject index to see how it is arranged. There may be an entry in this form:

County court
    jurisdiction
        extent

The general topic, County court, appears first, and later entries are progressively more specific. To use the index efficiently, you need to look under the general 'keyword' which will lead to the detailed answer to your problem rather than, as in this example, looking for an entry under Extent, which could be too specific to include a reference to county courts. A good index, however, will offer a variety of references, but finding the right one will always involve a process of elimination, and some inspired guesswork. Remember, however, that even in a legal textbook the 'keywords' need not be legal terms. The word 'money' may offer a more direct route to financial provision under the Child Support Act 1991 than the words 'matrimonial proceedings'.

2.5.2 Source index searches

Source indexes (also referred to as tables) may be indexes of statutes, statutory instruments or cases referred to in a work. They may be alphabetical, or chronological. They are most commonly used to find the text of the source (in a collection of primary sources), or commentary on the source (in a textbook). However, they have other uses too. Where you know the title of an Act, but not its date, or know the title of a case but not the law report reference, a source index can be used to complete the citation (see **4.1.2** and **4.2.2**). Obviously, an alphabetical index should be used for this purpose. If the date of the source is known but not the correct title, a chronological index may help. Sometimes, you can follow references to a source in order to find whether there have been later developments affecting it, for example a case interpreting a statute (see *Current Law* discussed at **5.3**).

2.6 UPDATING

2.6.1 A routine exercise

Developments occur even in the more sluggish backwaters of the law, and the practitioner must keep up to date. Updating research should therefore be a matter of routine, performed even where use of the sources of first resort seems to have produced a satisfactory answer. Here, as elsewhere, the essence of the skill of research is to be meticulous.

2.6.2 Likely developments

When updating, you should work out what developments are most likely to have occurred. You can then begin by checking for these. Is the area one which generates a large volume of case-law, affecting earlier cases, or the interpretation of a statute? Is it an area where the law can be changed by statutory instrument? Is it likely that new legislation has been enacted? Thorough updating will check for all these things, but the efficient researcher will check the most likely developments first.

2.6.3 General procedure

The particular procedure for updating will vary with the source used (see Chapters 3 and 4), but the following general points should be borne in mind.

(1) Begin by noting the information which is to be updated, with full references.
(2) In particular, note the date of the edition, issue or version in which the information was found.
(3) Stay with the source in which you found that information until it ceases to prove useful. For instance, if information has been found in a textbook, check whether any supplement has been issued.
(4) Check the date of information in any more recent source used.
(5) When switching sources, always check the database of the new source which may provide a different range of information from other sources used. If unfamiliar with its use, look for a user's guide, or a preface containing an explanation.
(6) Make notes of information and references during the investigation.

2.7 FURTHER READING

The Legal Research section of this Resource Book provides an introduction to the use of practitioner texts and collections of primary sources in Chapters 3, 4 and 5. Chapter 6 looks at the specialist sources available to the practitioner researching EC law, and Chapter 7 deals with electronic sources. However, it does not aim to be comprehensive. There are a growing number of works in this field, of which the following are particularly helpful.

Clinch *Using a Law Library* (Blackstone Press, 2000)
Dane and Thomas *How to Use a Law Library* (Sweet & Maxwell, 1996)
Warren *Legal Research in England and Wales* (Legal Information Resources, 1996)
Carpenter and Hodgson *Legal Research and the Law of the European Communities* (Legal Information Resources, 1997)

Stott *Legal Research* (Cavendish Publishing, 1998)
Tunkel *Legal Research* (Blackstone Press, 1992)

Chapter 3

CHECKING THE LAW

3.1 INTRODUCTION

The assumption to be made, for our present purposes, when dealing with library skills is that the principal has already completed an analysis of the relevant facts and made a preliminary legal analysis. The trainee's task is then to check the law so that he may confirm or alter his principal's preliminary legal analysis. When this is done, the trainee will look at primary sources to give final authority to that analysis.

Assume that you have identified the legal issues. You cannot normally begin your research by referring to primary sources. Even if your knowledge of the law in the particular area is substantial, it is normally wiser to begin the research by referring to a general statement of the law relating to the relevant issues, so as to gain a comprehensive overview of the applicable law. Ideally, such a general statement would be concise, yet comprehensive, dealing with points of fine detail, perhaps in appendices or footnotes, and containing detailed references to primary sources.

Such a general statement of the law is to be found in legal encyclopedias and practitioner textbooks. The first step is to check to see if there is an available practitioner textbook which covers the relevant area. If not, you should consult a legal encyclopedia, such as *Halsbury's Laws of England*, which gives an up-to-date coverage of the whole of the law of England and Wales. Either source should have an updating system, which should be used at this stage, as it is clearly important that your initial view of the law be as recent as possible. You must always check that your research is valid as at the date of your report.

3.2 PRACTITIONER BOOKS

The trainee will probably be more familiar with student textbooks than with practitioner works. In the office, you would not normally refer to student textbooks or other academic works, since their treatment of the subject would not necessarily assist a quick and practical assessment of the law relating to the issues. Furthermore, the practitioner textbook is likely to be extremely comprehensive and will also have the benefit of a detailed index.

You must check that the statement of law which you find is as up to date as possible. Publishers make various arrangements to keep such works up to date, and you must ensure that you understand how this is done in any book which you use. Publishers do not necessarily issue a new edition of a work each year (although this may occur in some subjects such as revenue law in which there are inevitably many changes of law each year and where an annual edition is justified).

The preface to the work will normally state the date up to which the law is correct. You should then check to see if a supplement has been published. Supplements are usually published annually and on a cumulative basis, so that earlier supplements need not be retained. Supplements are usually in paperback form.

Chapter 3 contents
Introduction
Practitioner books
Halsbury's Laws of England

A useful alternative to the updating problem is the loose-leaf system. Here the work is updated several times each year by the issue of supplements or 'Service Packs' containing new pages, with instructions for insertion of the new pages and removal of out-of-date pages. This is better than the use of an updating supplement where the researcher usually needs to search the supplement by means of a 'key' which will show whether a given page or paragraph number of the textbook is referred to in the supplement. In the loose-leaf system, changes in the law can be integrated into the main work itself. Furthermore, the greater frequency of issue of updating packs usually means that the loose-leaf work is more up to date than the textbook with its annual cumulative supplement. However, you must check that all supplements to a loose-leaf work have been filed. This can be done very quickly by checking the filing record kept in the book.

It is not possible to provide a comprehensive list of practitioner books, but examples include the following.

Criminal litigation

Archbold's Pleadings, Evidence and Practice in Criminal Cases (Sweet & Maxwell)
Blackstone's Criminal Practice (Blackstone Press)
Stone's Justices' Manual (Butterworth Law)

Conveyancing

Emmet on Title (Sweet & Maxwell)
Roper et al *The Law and Practice of Registered Conveyancing* (Sweet & Maxwell)
Law Society's Conveyancing Handbook (The Law Society)

Business

Butterworths Company Law Handbook
Lindley and Banks on Partnership (Sweet & Maxwell)

Tax

Butterworths Orange Tax Handbook
Butterworths Yellow Tax Handbook

Probate

Tristram and Coote's Probate Practice (Butterworth Law)

Mention should also be made of the precedent books which are available to the practitioner. They are used by practitioners to assist in the drafting of documents by giving examples of wording which can be adapted or adopted for use in a given matter. Annotations often explain the effect of particular wording, citing relevant authorities. Examples include:

Encyclopedia of Forms and Precedents (Butterworth Law)
Atkin's Court Forms (Butterworth Law)

3.3 HALSBURY'S LAWS OF ENGLAND

Halsbury's Laws of England is an encyclopedia which is now in its fourth edition. You should read the separate User's Guide which is supplied with the main volumes.

A search in *Halsbury's Laws* usually involves use of:

(1) the Consolidated Index;
(2) the main volumes;
(3) the annual Cumulative Supplement;
(4) the Current Service.

3.3.1 The Consolidated Index

It has been assumed that you have identified the legal issues which lie at the heart of the problem. It is crucial, now, to pick the word which is most likely to be used in an index to find the relevant statement of the law. This sounds obvious and yet proper use of an index is a skill in itself. You must accept that, if your original search word is unproductive, a better alternative must be found. A successful search in the Consolidated Index will produce both the relevant main volume number and a paragraph number. The Index does not give the relevant page number. If the paragraph number is followed by the letter 'n' with a small superscript number, this is a reference to a footnote to the paragraph which may refer to case-law and statutory or other sources. (If the Consolidated Index reveals nothing, use the subject indexes in the Cumulative Supplement and the Current Service – see **3.3.4** below.)

3.3.2 The main volumes

There are 52 main volumes, arranged alphabetically according to subject titles. Use of the Consolidated Index ensures that you refer to the appropriate main volume. However, in a straightforward case, where the issue and subject matter are clear-cut, you could simply go to the relevant main volume and use its own index.

3.3.3 Volumes 51 and 52

Main volumes 51 and 52 are concerned with aspects of European Community law which are relevant to English law. The index to both volumes is contained in Volume 52.

3.3.4 Updating

Where relevant material has been found by using the main volumes, it must be updated by use of the most recent annual Cumulative Supplement and the loose-leaf Current Service (in two binders updated monthly).

The procedure here is as follows:

(1) make a note of the edition, volume, title, paragraph and note number where the relevant information was found;
(2) find the latest Cumulative Supplement. This is issued annually, and updates the main work to 31 October each year;
(3) check the Cumulative Supplement for any entry identified by the reference in (1) above;

(4) find the loose-leaf Current Service binder. This will update for developments since 31 October of the previous year;
(5) check the Noter-up in the Current Service binder, for any entry identified by the reference in (1) above;
(6) if an entry is found, further detail will be found in the Monthly Reviews in the Current Service binder. This can be accessed by using the Cumulative Index and the Tables of Cases, Statutes and Statutory Instruments in that binder.

The Cumulative Supplement and Current Service can be used directly without first using the main work by use of the subject indexes. The subject index of the Cumulative Supplement is found at the end of Volume 2 of the Cumulative Supplement. The subject index for the Current Service is the Cumulative Index to the Monthly Reviews located in the Current Service binder. This would be appropriate where the researcher knew of a recent development which would not be noted in the main work, or where a search of the Consolidated Index does not reveal relevant material in the main work.

In addition, the Current Service provides sections covering recent material, inter alia, on commencement of statutes, personal injuries litigation, and interpretation of words and phrases.

A separate publication which may assist in updating is the annual Abridgment volumes. This covers the same material as the Current Service, but is published in hardback, and presents the developments for each calendar year. It may be useful if the researcher knows the year in which a development occurred.

3.3.5 Summary

The following diagram summarises the route for finding and updating material by use of *Halsbury's Laws*.

```
┌─────────────────────────────────┐
│     CONSOLIDATED INDEX          │
│       Volumes 55 & 56           │
└─────────────────────────────────┘
                │
┌─────────────────────────────────┐
│        MAIN VOLUMES             │
│ Volumes 1–50: Arranged by subject│
│   Volumes 51–52: EC Law         │
│   Volume 53: Table of Statutes  │
│   Volume 54: Table of Cases     │
└─────────────────────────────────┘
                │
┌─────────────────────────────────┐
│     CUMULATIVE SUPPLEMENT       │
│    Annual update to 31 October  │
└─────────────────────────────────┘
                │
┌─────────────────────────────────┐
│     CURRENT SERVICE BINDER      │
│           Noter-up              │
│         Monthly reviews         │
└─────────────────────────────────┘
```

Chapter 4

CITATION AND USE OF PRIMARY SOURCES

4.1 LEGISLATIVE MATERIALS

4.1.1 Introduction

Legal research can test any aspect of your working knowledge of the law, but it will make special demands on your knowledge of the categories of legal sources, and how to use them. This Resource Book does not aim to cover the same ground as academic texts on the legal system or legal method, but this section is designed to remind you of the basics. For further information on citation, see the works listed at **2.7**. On understanding legislative materials, the main practitioner work is Bennion *Statutory Interpretation*. On use of case-law, it is Cross and Harris *Precedent in English Law*.

4.1.2 UK statutes citation

The citation of statutes has varied throughout history. A number of citations may be given in respect of a single statute. The following is a short guide which will help to locate, in particular, older statutes.

1215–1548

Statutes for the period 1215–1548 were not cited individually but often by the name of the place where Parliament sat at the time. All legislation passed in one session is a 'statute'. Each individual 'Act' forms a separate chapter (abbreviated to 'ch' or 'c') but has no separate title. Today, an accompanying reference is usually given referring to the monarch and regnal year.

> *Example*
> 'Statute of Gloucester 1278 6 Edw. 1, c. 5' refers to an Act relating to tenancies and dilapidation.

1548–1963

From 1548 onwards, Acts are cited individually by reference to the Parliamentary session when they received Royal Assent, and by the regnal year.

A list of the regnal years and the corresponding calendar years can be found in Sweet & Maxwell's *Guide to Law Reports and Statutes*.

Often, an alternative 'short title' reference will be given. This is either in the Act itself ('this Act may be cited as …') or provided for in a Short Titles Act.

> *Example*
> '7 Wm IV and 1 Vict., c. 26' is the Wills Act 1837.

Chapter 4 contents
Legislative materials
Judicial decisions

Modern citations

The system of reference to regnal years was abolished with effect from 1 January 1963. Since then, statutes have been cited either by reference to their 'short title' or to their chapter number within a calendar year.

> *Example*
> 'Justices of the Peace Act 1979, c. 55', which is more usually referred to simply as the Justices of the Peace Act 1979.

Incomplete citations

Most statutes can be identified even from an incomplete citation. If a full citation is required, it can be found from several sources depending on the initial information. Always try the most obvious source first: a textbook, or practitioner work if the subject area is known. Other sources are as follows.

TITLE ONLY

Halsbury's Statutes has an annually published Tables of Statutes and General Index volume with an alphabetical list of all statutes passed. The most recent *Current Law Legislation Citator* has an alphabetical list of all post-1947 statutes and also pre-1947 statutes affected since that date (eg by repeal or case reference).

APPROXIMATE YEAR, INCOMPLETE TITLE

Halsbury's Statutes Tables of Statutes and General Index has a chronological list of statutes in force.

SUBJECT AREA ONLY

Use *Halsbury's Statutes* Tables of Statutes and General Index, which has a subject index to the volumes. Use *Halsbury's Statutes* loose-leaf Noter-up Service for more recent statutes.

For the use of *Halsbury's Statutes* generally, see Chapter 5.

4.1.3 Delegated (or subordinate) legislation

Delegated legislation is legislation made by a person or body other than Parliament. Generally, the authority for this lies in the 'parent' Act.

Examples are Regulations, Orders and procedural Rules.

Validity

Delegated legislation should be within the scope of the authority conferred (intra vires). If not, it can be challenged as being ultra vires.

Forms

Delegated legislation is generally made by statutory instrument and published by The Stationery Office.

Local authorities may have made by-laws. Copies of these are obtainable from them, for a fee.

Statutory instruments

To understand the terminology used in a statutory instrument (SI), it is useful to know something of the normal procedure for making them.

The relevant Minister 'makes' the Regulation or Order (ie it is drafted by a civil servant) and 'lays' it before Parliament. The instrument will state (after the title) the date when it was made, laid and, normally, when it comes into force, although the date may be contained in the body of the instrument. The instrument often has an explanatory note at the end of it which can provide useful cross-references.

CITATION

Statutory instruments are cited by year followed by numerical reference, for example: SI 1992/1758.

4.1.4 Understanding legislative materials

How thoroughly you research a problem involving a statute depends on the purpose of the research and the time available. If you need only to find an authority for a straightforward point, you can confine your research to the text only. If you are involved in litigation over the meaning of the statute, you must be more thorough and read the statute in its full context.

Even a quick check requires some skill. Remember that words used in an Act may be defined by the Act. Check for definitions sections which may cover relevant words. Remember also that one section or subsection may have to be read in the light of another. If a section begins 'Subject to section ...', always remember to check conditions or qualifications imposed in the other section. And always check that the text you are using is in force.

With the more thorough kind of research, the most important rule is to read the material as a whole. This means all the legislative materials, any relevant preparatory material such as Law Commission reports or possibly Hansard statements, and case-law interpreting the Act. The source material containing the text of the statute or statutory instrument, for example textbooks, practitioner works or *Halsbury's Statutes*, may refer to relevant case-law. Check each source date and update further from that, if necessary. See the example on interpretation of a statute at the end of this section.

One useful method of ensuring that the most up-to-date material is considered is to use the most recent *Current Law* Year Book, together with the latest Legislation Citator and Monthly Digest (see Chapter 5). In this way, you can find any development on a statute (whether by statute, statutory instrument or case-law). The Cumulative Index in each Year Book or Monthly Digest will refer to numbered paragraphs which should be consulted.

If you know that there is a reported case (or cases) on a statutory provision (and roughly the period), a quick check in the Index to the Law Reports may help. The volumes cover various periods (eg 1981–1990 cumulative, 1991–1998, 1999 and later updates) and cross-reference all cases reported in the major reports which considered any statutory provision (including statutory instruments). Look at the sections 'Statutes (or Statutory Instruments) Judicially Considered' which refers to each statute chronologically. An update would still be needed via the *Current Law*

Monthly Digest. Alternatively, try the Legislation Index in the Daily Law Reports index, which is even more up to date.

If a check is to be made on the interpretation of a particular word or phrase, cases can be checked, again using *Current Law*. *Stroud's Judicial Dictionary* is easy to use for individual words but again needs updating to ensure accuracy. *Words and Phrases Legally Defined* may also be useful.

Halsbury's Laws, Volume 44, Statutes, contains a useful summary of the rules of interpretation and construction, including definitions of certain words and phrases used in statutes.

Example

The Inheritance Tax Act 1984 contains the following provisions:

'**1. Charge on transfers**

Capital transfer tax shall be charged on the value transferred by a chargeable transfer.

2. Chargeable transfer and exempt transfers

(1) A chargeable transfer is a transfer of value which is made by an individual but is not (by virtue of Part II of this Act or any other enactment) an exempt transfer...

3. Transfers of value

(1) Subject to the following provisions of this Part of this Act, a transfer of value is a disposition made by a person (the transferor) as a result of which the value of his estate immediately after the disposition is less than it would be but for the disposition; and the amount by which it is less is the value transferred by the transfer...'

You may be surprised to discover that this provides authority for the proposition that inheritance tax may be charged on a lifetime gift to someone other than the donor's spouse. To interpret the provisions, it is necessary to unpack their meaning very carefully, checking whether each term used has been defined elsewhere, and whether each provision has to be read in the light of another.

Section 1 has to be read subject to s 100 of the Finance Act 1986, which says that references to capital transfer tax are to be read as references to inheritance tax. Section 1 also contains terms ('value transferred', 'chargeable transfer') which are meaningless without the further definitions contained in ss 2 and 3. The section does not refer you to these other provisions; you are left to check for yourself.

Sometimes the section contains a cross-reference. Section 2 refers you to exemptions contained in Part II of the Inheritance Tax Act, or any other Act. Section 3 is 'Subject to the following provisions of this Part'. This requires you to use the 'Arrangement of Sections' at the front of the Act to see what sections are contained in each Part. For example, Part I contains a group of sections under the cross-heading 'Dispositions which are not transfers of value'. You have to check these to understand the full effect of s 3, defining a 'transfer of value'.

You will obviously check for definitions of words which are otherwise meaningless. Be careful to check also for definitions of words which you think have a clear meaning. For example, the words 'disposition' and 'estate' in s 3 are given an extended meaning by the 'general interpretation section' (s 272). In the last resort, however, where the Act uses words (like 'individual') which are not further defined, you will have to trust your own interpretation.

On this basis, a lifetime gift of an asset is a 'transfer of value' within s 3(1). It is not chargeable if made to a spouse (one of the Part II exemptions referred to in s 2). Otherwise, it may be a 'chargeable transfer' subject to inheritance tax. (Whether inheritance tax is actually charged will depend on whether other exemptions apply, including the exemption for 'potentially exempt transfers' made 7 years before death, created by s 3A – the 'A' means that the section was inserted by a later Act, in this case the Finance Act 1986.)

When faced with a network of interrelated provisions like this, it is obviously prudent in practice to consult a practitioner text initially, and then to find a work (such as *Butterworths Orange Tax Handbook*) which annotates the statute, giving you any cross-references omitted from the text of the Act.

4.2 JUDICIAL DECISIONS

4.2.1 Citation of law reports

There are numerous sources for a report of a case. The most readily available sources are summarised below.

The Law Reports (1865–date)
In 1865, a Council of Law Reporting was set up to publish reports of important cases. In 1870, it became the 'Incorporated Council of Law Reporting for England and Wales'. The Council, which is controlled by the Inns of Court and The Law Society, produces reports known simply as the *Law Reports*.

The *Law Reports* are the 'semi-official' set of case reports. In each case report, counsel's argument is summarised and the judgment is revised by the judge before publication. The *Law Reports* reference is cited in preference to other reports.

A table of the modes of citation of these reports appears at the end of this chapter.

The Weekly Law Reports
Since 1953, the Council has also published the *Weekly Law Reports* ('the Weeklies'). In these case reports, counsel's arguments are not summarised and the judgments are not revised before publication.

Three volumes are published each year.

Volume 1 – Less important cases, not intended for republication in the *Law Reports*. This will include cases likely to go to appeal.

Volumes 2 and 3 – Cases likely to be published in the *Law Reports*, set out chronologically.

The Weeklies are first published in paperback and republished, indexed, in hardback at the end of the year.

Citation: *Wooldridge v Summer* [1962] 3 WLR 616.

The All England Law Reports

The *All England Law Reports* are a well-known and very reliable series of general reports. They are published weekly in paperback and republished, indexed, in hardback at the end of each year. Like the Weeklies, counsel's arguments are omitted and judgments are not revised. There are usually up to four volumes for each year, set out chronologically.

Citation: *R v Kelly* [1965] 2 All ER 250.

Specialist reports

There are numerous specialist reports including:

Criminal Appeal Reports (Cr App R)
Tax Cases (TC)
Road Traffic Reports (RTR)
Family Law Reports (FLR)
Industrial Tribunal Reports (ITR)
Estates Gazette Law Reports (EGLR).

Legal periodicals

Many legal periodicals contain law reports including:

Solicitors' Journal (Sol Jo), *New Law Journal* (NLJ) and *Criminal Law Review* (CrimLR) .

Newspapers

The Times and *The Independent*, for example, contain daily law reports.

Many law reports are cited by use of abbreviations. Most modern abbreviations can be found in *Current Law* (Monthly Digests, Year Books and Citators), *Halsbury's Laws*, Volume 1 and the Annual Supplement to the Digest. Raistrick's *Index to Legal Citations and Abbreviations* (Blackstone Press, 1993) gives a full list.

4.2.2 Incomplete citations

You may know the name of the case but not its citation (or you may need alternative citations to find an accessible report). Where the subject-matter is known, a check of the name in a textbook or practitioner book may give you the reference straightaway.

If this is unsuccessful or the subject matter is not known, the *Current Law* Case Citator is useful. This contains an alphabetical list of cases (of any date) reported or referred to in reported cases from 1947 onwards. Several references may be given. The citator will also note if this case was followed, distinguished or applied in subsequent cases. If the case is likely to be recent, check the case citator in the Monthly Digest.

For old cases, the *Law Reports* Index to the Digest of Cases could be used. It covers the period 1865–1950.

Other possible sources are the indexes to the major reports. For example, the *Law Reports* Index covers modern cases in several volumes. There are red hardback volumes for 1951–60, 1961–70, 1971–80 and 1981–90. A red paperback volume covers cases from 1991 to 1998, and another covers 1999. The most recent cases are indexed in a pink cumulative index published every few months. The title to the indexes is misleading. They cover cases reported in many other series, including the *All England Law Reports*.

The *All England Law Reports* provides Consolidated Tables and an Index, which indexes cases from 1936 onwards, but only those published in the *All England Law Reports*.

The *Current Law* Case Citator should give citations for all major reports but, especially with recent cases, the citations may not yet have appeared in *Current Law*. The *Daily Law Reports Index* is up to date to within a fortnight.

A check could also be made in *Halsbury's Laws* in the index to the relevant subject volume.

Note on case names

Although most cases are named in the form of *Smith v Jones*, it is worth being familiar with the other forms of case name. First, it helps for checking entries in tables and indexes. Secondly, it can throw light on the subject area and date of the case.

Smith v Jones

This is the usual form in civil cases, ie *Plaintiff* (or, now, *Claimant*) *v Defendant* (*Pursuer v Defender* in Scottish cases), or *Appellant v Respondent*. (However, this form could also refer to a criminal case in the magistrates' court, where the report is likely to be of an appeal to the Queen's Bench Divisional Court.)

R v Store (or Rex or Reg)

This is the usual form in criminal cases commencing in the Crown Court.

R v Secretary of State for the Home Department, ex parte Black

This is the usual form of name for applications for judicial review. The name given after the words 'ex parte' is that of the applicant, and as these cases are often known by that name, most (but not all) indexes provide cross-references from it.

Ex parte White

This form of name is usually where the report is on a point raised only at an ex parte hearing of one party, and the case does not proceed to trial between the parties; typically, nowadays, these are cases on application for leave to apply for judicial review.

Attorney-General, ex relatione Green v Sarum Borough Council

This is the form for a relator action to obtain relief in public law matters through the Attorney-General (likely to be pre-1977).

Re Boggis

Re Boggis, *In the goods of Boggis*, *Re Boggis Will Trusts* and *In the estate of Boggis* are used in wills and probate cases where the name cited is that of the deceased (although the executors or administrators brought the case before the court).

Re a company No 00034607 of 1990

This is likely to be a company insolvency case.

Re S (A Minor) (Care Proceedings: Wardship Summons)

In family law cases, the full name of the child cannot be given. The modern practice is to give the subject-matter of the case in parenthesis to help distinguish it from others.

Practice Direction (Family Court: Wardship Summonses)

Practice Directions are not case reports as such, but are published in the law reports. There are also Practice Notes, Practice Statements and, from the House of Lords, Procedure Directions.

The Hispaniola

This citation uses the name of a ship in a shipping case.

The post-Woolf system of civil justice may bring about changes in the naming of cases. The use of Latin terms, for example, seems unlikely to have a long-term future.

Chapter 5

FINDING PRIMARY SOURCES

5.1 LEGISLATIVE MATERIALS

5.1.1 Introduction

This chapter gives an introduction to the standard collections of primary sources and to some simple research tools available to the practitioner.

Remember the point made in Chapters 2 and 3 that it may be advisable to use a practitioner text to research a subject before looking at primary sources. A search may begin as a subject index search in a practitioner text, but once references have been found, it may then continue as a source index search in a collection of primary sources. Alternatively, you could begin with a subject index search in such a collection.

There are some golden rules here.

(1) Always check what the collection covers. Does it deal only with statutes, or also statutory instruments? With a collection of statutes, are there explanatory notes? If so, do they deal only with subsequent legislation, or also with cases interpreting the statutes?
(2) Work out the structure of the collection. Does it contain its own updating system? Some collections (eg Law Reports: Statutes) do not. Collections which update themselves commonly consist of a set of hardback main volumes which are revised every few years. These will then often be updated by an annual Supplement and a separate loose-leaf Service (sometimes called a Noter-up) which aims to catch the most recent developments. It is essential to check the date of the material you are using (see **2.6.3**).
(3) Check the possible access points, and work out which is most useful. Do you need a subject index or a source index? Is an alphabetical index of sources more useful than a chronological index? Is there any way of getting direct access to more recent materials (eg via a Service Index)?

5.1.2 Finding a statute

There are several ways to locate the text of a statute. The sources most readily available in practice are listed below. Remember, the text may have been amended and this must be checked.

Practitioner works
Practitioner works may contain the text, together with annotations, of relevant statutes. Also, they often contain subordinate legislation. Such specialist practitioner works are often neglected by student researchers in favour of more general works such as *Halsbury's Statutes* (see **5.1.3**) or *Halsbury's Statutory Instruments* (see **5.1.5**). However, while these general works are an invaluable tool, the specialist works can often be more convenient and equally authoritative sources of legislative material. You should use them when appropriate.

Chapter 5 contents
Legislative materials
Finding case-law
Current Law
Very recent developments

Many of these works are in loose-leaf form, and updated material is issued by the publishers. Check the latest update and make sure no amendments have been made since that date.

Annotated statutes

There are several texts of annotated statutes arranged either by year or subject. The most widely used annual texts are *Current Law* Statutes (1950–date) and *Butterworths Annotated Legislation Service* (1939–date). Bear in mind that an annual text will not cover any subsequent amendments.

Alternatively, *Halsbury's Statutes* is arranged in bound volumes by subject matter; for example, Treaties of the European Communities: Volume 50.

Halsbury's volumes are updated by reissue but cannot be fully up to date. It is necessary to use the Cumulative Supplement and Noter-up Service (see **5.1.3**). For very recent Acts, there is a loose-leaf Current Statutes Service. Repealed Acts or sections will not be reproduced when the volumes are reissued, but there will be a note of any repeal or amendment.

Other sources

Statutes of the Realm (1235–1713)
Public General Acts and Measures (1831–date)
Law Reports: Statutes (1866–date)

Official copies

Official copies of Acts can be purchased from The Stationery Office. This is useful when the text of a very recent Act is required. The publication of new Acts is reported in the *Daily List* of parliamentary publications, which also lists the commencement date of each statute.

Is it in force?

Check for any commencement section in the statute. It will usually be at the end. If there is none, the Act comes into force on the day of the Royal Assent. This date is in square brackets after the long title.

> *Example*
> Time Share Act 1992
>
> 1992 CHAPTER 35
>
> An Act to provide for rights to cancel certain agreements about time-share accommodation. [16 March 1992]

A commencement section may state a specific date or a 'day or days to be appointed'. Different sections of the Act may come into force on different days. A statutory instrument will be issued, usually bearing the title of the statute followed by '(Commencement) Order'. If several commencement orders have been issued they will be numbered. For example:

> 'Companies Act 1989 (Commencement No 3) Order 1990'.

To check commencement, see the latest volume of *Is it in Force?* (see **5.1.3**). The Noter-up Service must also be checked and, after the noter-up date, check *Current*

Law (see **5.3**) and the *Daily List* of parliamentary publications, issued by The Stationery Office.

Halsbury's Statutes also notes the commencement dates of all statutes up to the volume date. This is useful for pre-1966 statutes or when *Is it in Force?* is unavailable.

Halsbury's Statutory Instruments service contains an alphabetical list of recent commencement orders.

Legal periodicals such as the *New Law Journal*, the *Solicitors Journal* and the *Law Society Gazette* also note new commencement orders, but these are not necessarily comprehensive.

5.1.3 Halsbury's Statutes of England

Coverage

Halsbury's Statutes is a collection of all Public General Acts currently in force in England and Wales. It also contains some private and local Acts. It will not, however, give repealed Acts, and may not give the original text of an Act where it has been amended. It does not give the text of delegated legislation. It is, however, an annotated service giving brief notes on commencement (see **5.1.2**), amendments and repeals, cross-references to other provisions of the same or other Acts, judicial interpretation, and delegated legislation.

Structure and updating

Halsbury's Statutes consists of the following components.

MAIN VOLUMES

These are generally hardback volumes, arranged alphabetically according to subject matter. Each volume will deal with several titles. Within each title, Acts are set out in chronological order. If an Act deals with more than one subject, only part of it will appear under each relevant title.

Always check the date of the volume because there will have been a reissue if that title has been substantially affected by new legislation. This may, in fact, be more up to date than the Current Statutes Service.

CURRENT STATUTES SERVICE

This consists of loose-leaf binders containing recent statutes arranged in the same way as the main volumes.

ANNUAL CUMULATIVE SUPPLEMENT

This is a hardback volume published in April each year. It does not contain the text of statutes, but notes developments affecting statutes contained in the main volumes and Current Statutes Service. It would, for example, give details of any recent delegated legislation made under them. It is arranged according to the same titles, but with separate sections updating the main volumes and Current Statutes Service.

NOTER-UP SERVICE

This consists of a single loose-leaf binder updating the annual Cumulative Supplement and *Is it in Force?*.

IS IT IN FORCE?

Is it in force? is a separate paperback volume, published annually, giving the commencement date of every statute passed in the last 25 years.

Access

Halsbury's Statutes provides a number of different indexes, each serving a different purpose.

The Tables of Statutes and General Index is a paperback volume, published annually containing:

- an alphabetical list of statutes;
- a chronological list of statutes;
- a subject index for the main volumes;
- a subject index for the Current Statutes Service (giving access to more recent statutes).

There is a separate index to each main volume. This is useful if you already know the subject involved, but it will not cover developments after the date of the volume. In the case of a reissue volume, the index may be more up to date than the annual Tables of Statutes and General Index. However, you do have to be sure that the material you are looking for will be in that volume. The index will not refer you to relevant material in other volumes.

The most recent statutes, contained in the Current Statutes Service, may have been inserted after the date of the General Index. These can be accessed only by using the indexes in Binder A of the Current Statutes Service.

Using Halsbury's Statutes

The best advice on learning the use of *Halsbury's Statutes* is to spend a few hours in the library practising a range of search methods. It is beyond the scope of this Resource Book to describe all the permutations, but it may be helpful to outline the procedure for a typical search. The steps are illustrated below.

STEP 1 ⟶ STEP 2

GENERAL INDEX **VOLUMES 1–50**

contains – alphabetical list arranged by subject

– chronological list OR

– volume index* **CURRENT STATUTES SERVICE**

– service index* for recent statutes

(*by subject)

STEP 4 ⟵ STEP 3

NOTER-UP SERVICE **CUMULATIVE SUPPLEMENT**

most recent update annual update

[Note also *Is it in Force?*]

(1) Begin with the Tables of Statutes and General Index, and use either the source indexes or the subject indexes as appropriate. Note that there are two subject indexes, one covering the main volumes, and one covering the Current Statutes Service. It is a good idea to check both. Your search should give you either a main volume or Service (S) reference.

(2) Find the relevant main volume or Current Statutes Service binder; from the main volume, or Current Statutes Service, note the title of the volume, page number, title of the Act, section, subsection, or Schedule number, or note number, which is to be updated.

(3) Find the Cumulative Supplement. This will be up to date to 1 January of the year of the Supplement, but may note later developments. Check the Cumulative Supplement for any entry identified by the reference in (2) above.

(4) Find the loose-leaf Noter-up Service. This is normally updated three times per year. Check the date of the latest issue.

(5) Check the Noter-up for any entry identified by the reference in (2) above.

(6) To find the text of any statute referred to in the entry, use the Tables of Statutes and General Index. Other sources must be used to find the texts of cases or statutory instruments.

(7) If any new statute is found in the process of updating, it will be necessary to check whether it has come into effect.

5.1.4 Finding a statutory instrument

There is a vast number of statutory instruments (SIs). Every day, new ones are made and old ones repealed, and it can be very difficult to work out the current status of an SI. Official texts are published by The Stationery Office both separately and in annual volumes. Few libraries keep these. Most rely on *Halsbury's Statutory Instruments*. This hardback set of volumes is arranged alphabetically by subject matter and lists all SIs in force. It prints the full texts of selected SIs and summarises the rest. The two-volume loose-leaf service updates and cross-references the system (see **5.1.5**).

For even more recent SIs or amendments, the *Current Law* Monthly Digest will need to be checked. Very recent SIs will be noted in the legal periodicals and in the *Daily List* of parliamentary publications from The Stationery Office. Individual copies of the text would have to be purchased from The Stationery Office.

The texts of SIs may also be found in practitioner works.

Electronic sources are useful as they allow easy access to the full text of all statutory instruments.

5.1.5 Halsbury's Statutory Instruments

Coverage

As explained in **5.1.4**, *Halsbury's Statutory Instruments* lists all SIs currently in force, printing the full text of some SIs and summarising the rest. Like *Halsbury's Statutes*, it will not give the text of repealed instruments but does contain useful annotations which should always be checked.

Structure and updating

Halsbury's Statutory Instruments consists of the following components.

MAIN VOLUMES

The main volumes are arranged in a similar way to *Halsbury's Statutes*, alphabetically according to subject matter, with SIs in each volume set out in chronological order. Again, the reissue system is used, with volumes being replaced individually as the material becomes out of date.

THE UPDATING SERVICE

This consist of two loose-leaf binders. The Service binder contains the following:

(i) the Chronological List of Instruments. If you know the SI reference, this will tell you under which title it is included;
(ii) the alphabetical list of SIs. This is useful if you know only the SI title;
(iii) the Table of Statutes. If you know the Act under which the SI was made, this will again give you the title covering any relevant SIs;
(iv) the list of Commencement and Appointed Day Orders for statutes;
(v) the Monthly Update. This notes changes by reference to the main volumes, and in the same order. It is updated monthly. It contains lists and summaries of new instruments, and a noter-up section adding to the annotations in the main volume.

The second binder contains Additional Texts – full texts of some recent instruments not given in the main volumes. The annual Cumulative Supplement and the Monthly Update may refer you to these texts.

ACCESS

The main indexes are contained in a separate paperback volume issued annually. This contains a Consolidated Index which enables you to search by subject, and an alphabetical list for use when you know the title of the SI. If you already know the SI number, use the Chronological List in the Service binder.

In addition, each main volume has a subject index, for direct access if you are certain which title is relevant. For recent changes, there is a monthly index to each Service Binder.

Using Halsbury's Statutory Instruments

STEP 1 ⟶ STEP 2

CONSOLIDATED INDEX   **VOLUMES 1–22**

subject index   arranged by subject

alphabetical list of SI titles

STEP 3

MONTHLY UPDATE

contained in Service Binder 1

Note

Full text of most important recent SIs in Additional Texts (Service Binder 2)

Key lists most recent SIs and notes amendments/revocations

Summaries of most recent SIs

Once again, the best way to learn how to use *Halsbury's Statutory Instruments* is by practice. Many different search routes are available, but it may be helpful to describe the course of a typical search. The steps are illustrated below.

(1) Begin with the Index volume and use either the subject index or the alphabetical index as appropriate. This should give a main volume reference. If it gives a Service Binder (S) reference, go to step (3).
(2) Find the relevant main volume; note the title of the SI and the title and number of the volume, and page number where it was found.
(3) Find the Monthly Update in the looseleaf service and check it for any entry identified by the reference in (2) above.

Instead of checking against the page reference in steps (3) and (4), you may use the Amendments and Revocations section, checking against the SI number.

5.1.6 Statute-related rules

Statute-related rules may be materials not enacted as legislation but of importance to it, such as circulars issued by Ministers on green belt policies in planning law.

These circulars, guidelines, etc may be published by and obtained from The Stationery Office or the government department. Practitioner works may also contain them.

5.1.7 EC legislation

UK legislation has to be read in conjunction with any relevant EC law (see Chapter 6).

5.2 FINDING CASE-LAW

The most effective way to find case-law on a subject is to use the subject index of a practitioner text, or *Halsbury's Laws of England*, and look for references in the text (see Chapter 3). If you know the year of a case, you could use the subject index of the *Current Law* Year Book for that year (see **5.3**). Similarly, if you think that there may be a recent case, you can use the *Current Law* Monthly Digest. Electronic sources can be a very efficient way of searching by subject (see Chapter 7).

Once you have the correct citation, you can go straight to the text of the case. For incomplete citations, see **4.2.2**.

Always remember to check whether a case has been subsequently distinguished or overruled (eg by using the *Current Law* Case Citator, see **5.3**).

5.3 CURRENT LAW

5.3.1 What is *Current Law*?

Current Law is the most general updating source available. It consists of the *Current Law* Citators, the Monthly Digest, and the Year Books (which consolidate the Monthly Digest). *Current Law* Statutes Annotated is a separate, self-contained service.

Current Law is not a collection of primary sources. The Year Books and Monthly Digest give only notes on developments. However, its value is that it deals with all types of developments, statutes, SIs and case-law. It can be used either to update research from other sources, or to check for recent developments in any area.

5.3.2 The *Current Law* Citators

The *Current Law* Citators can be used to check post-1947 developments (including developments affecting earlier legislation and cases). These include a Case Citator, a Legislation Citator and now a separate Statutory Instruments Citator. The most recent citators are now available electronically.

THE CASE CITATOR

The use of the Case Citator to find the citation of a case and to check how it has been dealt with in later cases is described in **4.2.2**. There are three hardback volumes (1947–76, 1977–88, 1989–95). Developments in 1996 and 1997 are covered in one paperback volume. You will need to check the December monthly parts for 1998 and 1999 and the latest issue for 2000 to bring yourself up to date. Updating procedure involves finding the volume in which the case is first noted, and then checking the case lists in later volumes (and the latest monthly part) for subsequent developments. The Citator gives the paragraph in the Year Book where the development is reported.

THE LEGISLATION CITATOR

The use of the Legislation Citator to find a statute is described in **5.1.2**. It can also be used to check for amendments, repeals, and cases interpreting the statute. Again, there are three hardback volumes plus a paperback volume. Updating procedure involves finding the volume where the statute is first noted. It will be found listed in chronological order, with separate notes on each section. The later volumes must also be checked for subsequent developments. The most recent developments are covered in a paperback booklet issued bi-monthly with the Monthly Digest.

```
HARDBACK VOLUME OF FIRST REFERENCE
              ↓
         LATER VOLUMES
              ↓
       LATEST MONTHLY PART
```

If the Legislation Citator tells you that there has been a case which interprets the statute, you should use the Case Citator to update the case.

This diagram shows the usual procedure for updating a case (using the Case Citator).

For updating a statute, the procedure is the same except that, instead of finding the latest Monthly Part, you should look for the booklet containing the Legislation Citator for the current year.

THE STATUTORY INSTRUMENTS CITATOR

This covers developments from 1993 onwards, affecting all SIs. It aims to enable you to find out, for example, whether an SI has been amended or revoked by an SI or a statute issued after 1992, and whether any post-92 cases have involved the application of any SI. If you are checking for recent developments, the procedure is:

(1) note the year and SI number of the SI in question;
(2) use this reference to check the hardback Citator volume covering the years from 1993 to 1995, then the paperback for 1996–98, December 1999 and the latest monthly issue;
(3) update using the loose-leaf *Current Law* Statutes Service (issued bi-monthly).

5.3.3 The Monthly Digest

The Monthly Digest can be used in a number of different ways.

UPDATING THE CASE CITATOR

The final stage in tracing the history of a case will be to check the Cumulative Table of Cases in the Monthly Digest covering the years not covered in the latest Case Citator. The Digests are cumulative for each year, so it is only necessary to check the December issue for a completed year, and the latest issue for the current year. The entry will refer to the month of, and note number in the Monthly Digest in which the development was reported.

UPDATING THE LEGISLATION CITATOR

The final stage in checking legislative developments will be to check the latest Legislation Citator for the current year (issued with the Monthly Digests but in booklet form).

The procedure for checking is as follows:

(1) note the title, regnal year and chapter of the Act in question, and the section or Schedule being checked;
(2) check the current year's Legislation Citator for an entry identified by the reference in (1);
(3) for the text of the development, use other sources. A note on the development may be found in the Monthly Digests. This can be accessed by using the Case Table, alphabetical list of SIs, or subject index, as appropriate.

CHECKING RECENT DEVELOPMENTS BY SUBJECT HEADING

Some recent developments may not be reported as developments of earlier cases or statutes. Updating is complete only if you check for such developments by using the Cumulative Index in *Current Law*. The procedure here is as follows:

(1) find the latest issue of the Monthly Digest;
(2) check the list of subject headings at the beginning, and identify the heading to be researched;
(3) turn to the Cumulative Index. Check under the heading identified in (2) for any reference to the topic to be researched;
(4) check the December issue for the previous year, or the Year Book if published, using the same method. Always check the headings in use for the particular volume;
(5) check earlier Year Books if necessary.

OTHER USES

The Monthly Digest also contains up-to-date information on quantum of damages for personal injuries, words and phrases judicially considered, High Court fees, progress of Bills in Parliament, dates of commencement of statutes, and a very useful list of the abbreviations used in citations of cases and journals.

5.4 VERY RECENT DEVELOPMENTS

No matter how thorough the research, there will always be a possibility that developments have occurred in the period since the last available information was published. Even with *Current Law*, six weeks may elapse before developments are noted. One approach is to take comfort in the fact that, if all available sources have been checked, no other practitioner is likely to know of a development either.

Possible sources for latest developments are:

(1) the weekly journals including the *New Law Journal*, the *Solicitors Journal* and the *Law Society Gazette* (accessed via the *Legal Journals Index*);
(2) specialist publications in the field in question, for example *Simon's Tax Intelligence*;
(3) for statutory instruments, the *Daily List* of Stationery Office publications;
(4) daily law reports in the national newspapers (accessed via the *Daily Law Reports Index*);
(5) electronic databases.

5.4.1 The Legal Journals Index

Coverage

The *Legal Journals Index* (*LJI*) covers all journal titles published in the UK which are devoted to law or frequently contain legal articles.

Structure

LJI is published monthly, and cumulated both quarterly (in paperback) and annually (in hardback). It is also available electronically.

Access

There are five separate indexes in *LJI*: a subject index, an author index, a case index, a legislation index, and a book review index.

When would you use *LJI*? Obviously, the journals indexed usually contain commentary or summaries of legal developments rather then the full text of cases or statutes, but *LJI* is particularly useful for very recent developments when the full text has not yet become available, and for checking the practical significance of developments. This can be more helpful to the practitioner than finding the primary source itself.

5.4.2 The Daily Law Reports Index

Coverage

The *Daily Law Reports Index* (*DLRI*) indexes reports in various newspapers, particularly *The Times*, and the *Independent*.

Structure

DLRI is published weekly in loose-leaf format, cumulated quarterly into a paperback, and annually in hardback volumes. It is available electronically.

Access

DLRI contains six indexes: a Parties index – just an alphabetical index without text; a case index – the same but with a summary of the case; a keyword index enabling you to search by subject; a legislation index enabling you to check recent developments affecting particular statutes; a ship's names index – for shipping law specialists who may know the name of the ship but not that of the case; and (quarterly only) a cumulative case report index which tells you where to find a full case report (for example in the *Weekly Law Reports*).

When would you use *DLRI*? Obviously, it is just an index. It does not add anything to the cases reported in the dailies, although it may help you locate a known case more quickly. However, it is of great assistance in locating cases you do not know about – when you are looking for recent developments in a particular area, or affecting a particular statute. It is more up to date than *Current Law*, although its coverage is more limited.

Chapter 6

EC LAW

6.1 INTRODUCTION

6.1.1 General research

Research into the law of the European Community is not a task for the faint-hearted. The difficulty of keeping up with the flood of legislation and case-law emanating from Brussels, Luxembourg and Strasbourg is compounded by the fact that much of the material takes a considerable time to filter through the traditional sources. Specialist EC practitioners thus become adept at using all manner of different research methods in their search for proposals which will influence their clients' business decisions: contact with government departments, for instance, may give an instant updating on the development of a particular piece of legislation, thus providing a service which no traditional source can offer.

6.1.2 Library sources

Whilst the importance of entrepreneurial research in the field of EC law cannot be underestimated, the student researcher will first need to be acquainted with the essential library sources. This brief introduction to research into EC law aims to familiarise the student with those sources; after reading this chapter and practising his new skills, the researcher should be able to track down references to EC legislation and case-law and, as a necessary adjunct, begin to develop a feel for spotting the 'Europoint' in a file, even if no such point seems at first sight to be in issue.

It is assumed that the researcher already has a basic knowledge of EC law. Although brief references to certain substantive points of law are inevitable, so far as possible they have been kept to a minimum.

6.1.3 *Vaughan: Law of the European Communities Service*

Although it is beyond the scope of this Resource Book to deal with the vast number of secondary works covering EC law, you should be aware of this work, published by Butterworths in four loose-leaf volumes.

Under 23 subject headings, it gives you commentary on the whole of EC law, with lists of legislation and separate tables and indexes for each heading.

If you need to perform a subject search, or find a general explanation of an area of EC law before researching primary sources, it is a good idea to begin with *Vaughan*.

Chapter 6 contents
Introduction
Primary legislation
Secondary legislation
Information on proposed legislation
Case-law
CELEX

6.2 PRIMARY LEGISLATION

6.2.1 Substance

The primary legislation of European Community Law comprises the following.

(1) The founding treaties which set up the three European Communities. These are:
   (a) the Treaty of Paris 1951, establishing the European Coal and Steel Community (ECSC);
   (b) the Treaty of Rome 1957, establishing the European Atomic Energy Community (EURATOM); and
   (c) the Treaty of Rome 1957, establishing the European Economic Community (EEC).

(2) The treaties and Acts which amend the three founding treaties; these include the Brussels Merger Treaty 1965; the Single European Act 1986; the Treaty on European Union 1992 (the Maastricht Treaty); and the Treaty of Amsterdam 1997.

(3) The accession documents of new Member States, including the 1972 Accession Treaty under which the UK, Denmark and Ireland joined the EC.

6.2.2 Sources of primary legislation

Updated texts of the treaties themselves and the most important of the other primary legislation can be found in:

(1) *Encyclopedia of European Community Law* (Sweet & Maxwell). This encyclopedia is gradually being replaced by the *Encyclopedia of European Union Law*. The text of the treaties and other primary legislation is now to be found in those five volumes of the replacement work which are entitled *Constitutional Texts*.
(2) *Halsbury's Statutes* (Butterworth Law, 4th edn, Vol 50).
(3) *Basic Community Laws* (6th edn) edited by Rudden and Wyatt (OUPR). The treaties and related primary legislation are contained in Part 1.

6.3 SECONDARY LEGISLATION

6.3.1 Substance

The secondary legislation of the EC comprises Acts made by the Council of Ministers and the Commission under the powers granted to them in the treaties.

This legislation has binding force insofar as it consists of:

(1) Regulations, which are binding in their entirety and directly applicable. No further implementation by Member States is needed for Regulations to have effect.
(2) Directives, which are binding only as to the result to be achieved but which leave Member States a choice of the form and manner of implementation.
(3) Decisions, which are binding in their entirety on the Member States or individuals to whom they are addressed.

Alternatively, the legislation may be non-obligatory and take the form of a Recommendation or an Opinion.

6.3.2 Citation of secondary legislation

The researcher's first hurdle in tracing secondary legislation is coming to terms with the rather obscure methods of citation, methods which derive from 1968 when the Official Journal of the EC (see below) was split into two series.

Regulations

Regulations are cited as: Reg (EC) 2349/84

After the abbreviation of the Regulation comes the name of the Community from which it derives, bracketed: here it is the European Economic Community. There follows the number of the Regulation in the year, here 2349. Finally comes the year, 1984.

Decisions and Directives

Confusingly for the uninitiated, Decisions and Directives are cited quite differently: Dir 89/592/EEC.

Here, after the abbreviation, Dir, comes the year of issue, 1989, followed by the number of the Directive in the year, 592. The relevant Community comes at the end, unbracketed.

6.3.3 Source

The texts of all secondary legislation can be found in the Official Journal of the European Community (the 'OJ' or, in French, 'JO'). Appearing as it does almost every day, the OJ provides regularity of service for the Euro-insomniac, but is generally regarded as an irksome document for the researcher to grapple with, particularly because of some deficiencies in its index.

The OJ is published in two main series:

(1) the 'L' series 'Legislation'; and
(2) the 'C' series 'Communications and Information'.

The 'L' series contains all EC legislation and is itself subdivided into two parts. First, there are the Acts whose publication is obligatory under the treaties, ie Regulations and ECSC Decisions. Secondly, there are those whose publication is not obligatory, ie all other legislation. Indications of particularly important legislation are given by the use of bold type and, on the contents page, by asterisks.

The 'C' series is used to disseminate a variety of categories of information, and a quick look through on a daily basis will keep the researcher in touch with the following: draft legislation; European Parliament opinions on draft legislation; decisions of the European Court of Justice (ECJ) (but not the texts of the judgments); and recent requests for rulings in the ECJ.

Citations to the OJ are relatively straightforward giving the year, series, issue number and page. Thus, 'OJ 1988 L50/18' is the 'L' series OJ, issue number 50, page 18. In some law reports this would appear as '[1988] OJ L50/18'. Sometimes, the precise date of the OJ in question will also be cited.

6.3.4 Tracing secondary legislation

Encyclopedia of European Community Law

The volumes marked 'C' (Numbers I to XI) of *Encyclopedia of European Community Law* (Sweet & Maxwell) contain a wide selection of the most important secondary legislation. The volumes are subdivided into Parts referred to by the letter 'C' followed by an arabic number. Thus, for example, C17 is the Part concerned with environmental legislation: this Part can be found in Volume XI of the 'C' volumes.

Tracing secondary legislation with a citation

Assuming a citation is to hand, the simplest approach to tracing secondary legislation is to turn to the checklist in Part C18 of Volume XI. This lists all the secondary legislation held in the *Encyclopedia*. The list begins with the Regulations, in chronological order: it continues with the Decisions, Directives, Recommendations and Opinions, all intermingled but again in chronological order. The citation is on the left-hand side of the page, and the reference on the right.

> *Example*
> Assume that you have a citation for Directive 89/48 of 1989 (the Mutual Recognition of Higher Education Diplomas Directive). This Directive can be traced in the second half of the checklist, remembering that it is Directive Number 48 of 1989: the text is in Part C12 (which happens to be in Volume VII) at paragraph 885.

Tracing secondary legislation without a citation

There are two possible approaches to the problem of tracing secondary legislation without a citation: either to use the index in Volume XI, or, alternatively, to second-guess the subject matter, go directly to the relevant Part and scan through the list of contents at the beginning of the Part.

The starting point will usually be the index, but this is not always as useful as it might be. Thus, only by searching 'Diplomas' or 'Education' would you find the Directive 89/48: neither 'Recognition' nor 'Mutual Recognition' would have thrown up the reference: given that the Directive is entitled 'the Mutual Recognition of Higher Education Diplomas', you might have expected those words to have triggered some reaction.

Consequently, a quick look through the list of legislation at the beginning of Part C12, the 'Right of Establishment' section, might have traced the Directive more quickly.

6.3.5 Checking the status of secondary legislation

'Current Status'

EC legislation may be amended or repealed, and therefore an up-to-date guide to the current status of such legislation is an invaluable aid to the researcher. *European Communities Legislation: Current Status* performs this function. It is published annually in two hardback volumes which are backed up by supplements appearing each May, August and November: each supplement contains an updated index to the complete work.

The hardback volumes are split chronologically, the first covering the period 1952–1980, and the second 1981–date. Each volume is subdivided into years and, within each year, the Regulations and ECSC Decisions are listed first (in the manner of the OJ), followed by the remainder of the secondary legislation. Having traced the legislation, it is possible to see straightaway: whether it is still in force or spent; what amendments and repeals have been made to it; and a brief description of its content.

If no citation is available for the legislation in question, it can be traced using the index of the latest supplement. The entries to the index of this work are based on Community phraseology used in titles to the acts as well as terms in common usage. Thus, to trace the Mutual Recognition of Diplomas Directive, a search under 'Diplomas' will lead to 'Right of establishment and freedom to provide services — mutual recognition of diplomas' 89/48 and 89/49. This will, in turn, lead on to the status of those Directives in Volume 2. A further check on recent developments should then be made in the most recent cumulative supplement.

A telephone facility is also available providing the latest available information in this field.

6.3.6 Checking to see if a Directive has been incorporated into UK law

General

Directives are only binding as to the effect to be achieved, and governments of Member States are left to implement EC legislation by incorporation into national law. In the case of the UK, this will be achieved by statute or, more commonly, statutory instrument.

When researching a Directive, it is important to know if national legislation has, in fact, been passed to implement it and, if so, what that legislation is.

Butterworths EC Legislation Implementator

A one-volume book entitled *Butterworths EC Legislation Implementator* appears twice yearly. It is divided into two sections: the first lists, in chronological order, all Directives which have been implemented by UK legislation, with the target date for implementation and a reference to the relevant UK legislation alongside. Thus if, for example, the researcher wishes to know whether Directive 89/48 (as to Mutual Recognition of Diplomas) has been put into effect in UK law, it could be seen immediately that there was a target date of 4 January 1991 for implementation; furthermore, the relevant UK legislation is the Education (Teachers) Regulations 1989, SI 1989/1319 and the EC (Recognition of Professional Qualifications) Regulations 1991, SI 1991/824. You would need to refer to, say, *Halsbury's Statutory Instruments* for the actual texts of those instruments.

The second section of the book reproduces the latest table from the Annual Report to the European Parliament, listing the Member States which have implemented particular Directives. Considerable care is needed here since the table will usually be out of date.

6.3.7 Other sources for keeping up to date with secondary legislation

European Current Law is a monthly journal published towards the end of every month with a cumulative index in each supplement. It contains short details of the most important EC legislation, as well as important legislation recently enacted nationally within European (EC and non-EC) countries. The supplements are bound together annually into a hardback volume.

Current Law and *Halsbury's Laws*, which are discussed in **5.2**, contain references to the most important EC legislation.

6.4 INFORMATION ON PROPOSED LEGISLATION

6.4.1 Tracing draft legislation

Brief mention was made in **6.1** of the importance of keeping abreast of proposed legislation. As a result of this demand, there are several specialised services which provide regular up-to-date information on European matters for their subscribers. The researcher who does not have the benefit of such a subscription may have to be satisfied with the following sources.

6.4.2 *European Access*

European Access is a bi-monthly bulletin which covers a selection of draft Commission proposals which have not yet been published in the OJ. Such proposals are known as COM documents and are cited accordingly with number and year, followed by the word 'FINAL', which indicates that the draft is a final draft. Generally, earlier drafts will not be within the public domain.

6.4.3 The Official Journal

Draft legislation will appear in the OJ when the Commission seeks an opinion from the European Parliament and the Economic and Social Committee. Further amended drafts may follow. The problem, as ever, with the OJ is the lack of an adequate index for tracing this material.

6.4.4 Other sources

Up-to-date information can often be obtained from the London offices of the European Commission Information Support Unit (tel 020 7973 1992) and the European Parliament (tel 020 7222 0411) and via their Internet sites. The Commission operates an open-door policy so that a telephone call to the official dealing with proposed legislation may save hours of painstaking research. The relevant officials (and telephone numbers) are listed in the Directory of the Commission of the European Community, published by the Community but available from The Stationery Office. Furthermore, for those on its mailing list, the Commission also publishes free weekly bulletins of the week's developments as well as booklets setting out Commission policy in areas such as competition, environmental and consumer law.

The *Financial Times* has an excellent European service, and topical information can be obtained from that newspaper.

6.5 CASE-LAW

6.5.1 The courts

Proceedings before the European Courts will be heard in:

(1) the Court of Justice of the European Communities (the 'ECJ'); or
(2) the Court of First Instance of the European Communities, established by the Single European Act of 1986.

Additionally, there will be many cases heard in the national courts of the Member States which are of importance to the EC law researcher.

6.5.2 Citation of EC cases

Cases in the ECJ

ECJ cases are cited with their names and, additionally, their numbers. A case may thus be cited as *British Aerospace and Others v EC Commission* C292/90. The letter 'C' (short for 'Cour') indicates this to be an ECJ case: furthermore, it is the Case number 292 of 1990. It is important to remember that the year in the citation refers to the year when the case was filed, rather than the year of the decision. This can cause endless confusion.

Cases in the Court of First Instance

First instance cases are cited in the same way as those in the ECJ except that the number is prefixed by the letter 'T' (short for 'Tribunal') instead of 'C'.

6.5.3 The law reports

The ECR

The Official Law Reports are called Reports of Cases before the Court (ECR). Since the reports have to be translated from French into all the official languages of the EC, it is usual to have to wait 2 years or so before a report appears in the ECR. Needless to say, researchers look for other means of obtaining essential information from the cases, and one can usually acquire copies of the judgments and opinions of the Advocate-General from the Court Registry. There is a subscription service for such material. Hardy souls who can deal with the reports in French have an advantage since they will often appear in that language first.

Common Market Law Reports (CMLR)

The Common Market Law Reports are an unofficial series of reports which appear monthly and contain a selection of ECJ and first-instance decisions, together with certain Commission Decisions and reports of cases before the courts of member states which have a bearing on EC law. These reports are bound at the end of the year and cited as follows: [1981] 2 CMLR 362.

This refers to Volume 2 of the CMLR of 1981 at page 362.

There is now also a separate Anti-Trust Supplement to the CMLR dealing only with Competition cases; these are hived off into separate volumes, but are cited in the same way as other reports. As well as decisions of the Commission, CFI and ECJ the Anti-Trust Supplement to the CMLR includes Commission notices and legislation such as block exemptions.

The Official Journal

The 'C' series of the *Official Journal* will give indications of orders and judgments made in the courts, but nothing more. Indication that judgment has been given, however, will tell the researcher that the Court Registry should have the judgment available within one month or so.

Other sources

A number of important decisions are reported in the law reports contained in newspapers (especially *The Times* and Tuesday's edition of the *Financial Times*). *Current Law* and *Halsbury's Laws* also provide summaries of the most important cases on a monthly basis. The *European Court Monitor* (published by the European Law Press) which appeared in 1996 gives shortened reports of all ECJ and CFI cases, it appears six times per year and may be the most reliable method of keeping up to date until the full report appears.

6.5.4 The All England Law Reports

Since January 1996, the All England Law Reports have produced a monthly series of European Cases. The citation here is [1996] All ER (EC) 301. As with all ECJ cases, be careful of joined cases. Hence *Factortame*, the important recent case on damages against States, is not cited in the index but is reported as *Brasserie au Pecheur SA v Germany* [1996] All ER (EC) 301.

6.6 CELEX

CELEX contains the official legal database of the European Community in electronic format. It includes the text of the treaties and other legislation as well as judgments of the European Court of Justice, proposals and details of national implementation.

Chapter 7

THE ELECTRONIC LAW LIBRARY

7.1 INTRODUCTION TO ELECTRONIC MATERIALS

7.1.1 What is available?

Not all law libraries consist of printed materials alone; they are increasingly being supplemented (and, indeed, being overtaken) by 'electronic libraries' where material is either held within or accessed through a computer system. There are two major sources of electronic information: CD-ROMs and on-line databases. You may well find that an electronic source (often an electronic version of a well-established paper one) has become your normal research tool, supplemented on occasion by paper sources, rather than the other way around.

A CD-ROM is a compact disk which holds a bank or 'databases' of information. They are portable and transferable from one personal computer to another (as long as each computer has a drive suitable for reading the information from the disk). On-line information, however, is where your computer is linked to another computer and the information is read or transferred down the phone line; in other words, the information is held 'remotely'. On-line information is usually more up to date than CD-ROM. Often, the same services are offered on CD-ROM and via the Internet. The two versions of this service are not always identical, if only because on-line information is usually more up to date. When you are assessing a CD-ROM source via an internal network, set up within your particular office or library, you may find that you are scarcely aware of the difference between this and the equivalent Internet source.

7.1.2 Advantages and disadvantages of electronic libraries

There are a number of advantages to using electronically held information:

(1) the sheer quantity of information which can be stored in such a small area and retrieved at the touch of a button greatly exceeds what a paper library could supply;
(2) material can be kept up to date more easily than rewriting a whole book;
(3) relevant items can be located far more quickly than with paper sources as the computer is often able to scan all the text in a database to retrieve 'matches' to limited information, such as a half-remembered case name or phrase from a judgment;
(4) there is less reliance on other forms of communication, such as the postal service, as information, for example data from the other side of the world, can be seen instantly by using the internet.

Some of the disadvantages of electronically held information are:

(1) there will always be a cost with on-line information, as the Internet must be used to connect to the remote database;

Chapter 7 contents
Introduction to electronic materials
Introduction to CD-ROMs
Introduction to on-line materials

(2) some systems are not user-friendly and will require training prior to information retrieval;

(3) there is always a risk of network or personal computer failure.

7.1.3 Conducting a search

When using electronic sources of information, there are seven basic commands whose function is universal (although not all electronic products allow use of all of them). These commands are often referred to as 'boolean operators'. The seven basic boolean operators are **and**, **or**, **not**, **within/of**, **near**, * (the asterisk), and ! (the exclamation mark).

AND – this command will combine two terms so they both appear in the same paragraph or document. The **and** command is used to narrow down a search:

    eg donoghue **and** stevenson

OR – the **or** command will allow you to expand a search, for example if using terms which have synonyms:

    eg fence **or** boundary **or** perimeter

NOT – the **not** command allows searching for a term(s), but with the exclusion of another term:

    eg (licences **and** alcohol) **not** children

WITHIN/OF – this command lets you narrow down the search of two or more terms so that they are within a specified number of words away from each other:

    eg contract **within** 5 **of** termination

NEAR – the **near** command is similar to the **within/of** command, but it has a default value which ensures that the terms are likely to be in the same paragraph:

    eg gambling **near** lottery

* – the asterisk symbol is the most commonly used truncation or wildcard symbol, and is used to allow a variety of endings on a particular term to expand the search possibilities:

    eg neglige* (will find: negligent, negligence, negligently and negligee)

! – the exclamation mark is used as a wildcard symbol, but in the middle of a word, and can be used if the researcher is unsure of the spelling or it can be used instead of the **or** command:

    eg wom!n (will find women or woman).

However, it is important to remember that the computer is not intelligent and, in most products, if you type in a phrase, it will search exactly for that phrase.

7.2 INTRODUCTION TO CD-ROMS

7.2.1 What is available on CD-ROM?

Increasing numbers of legal CD-ROMs are becoming available which are aimed at legal practitioners.

JUSTIS – published by Context Ltd, the CD-ROMs produced under the JUSTIS title include the full text of the *Weekly Law Reports*; the full text of the Law Reports on the *Electronic Law Reports*; the full text of *Family Law Reports*; and the *CELEX* CD-ROM, which is the official database of the European Community, comprising the text of treaties, EC legislation, case-law, summaries of proposed legislation, and the DTI Spearhead database.

Butterworths Books on Screen (BOS) – some titles included in the BOS series are: *All England Law Reports*; *Civil Court Practice* and *Butterworths County Court Precedents and Pleading*; *Encyclopaedia of Forms and Precedents*; *Inland Revenue Manuals*; and *Harvey on Industrial Relations*.

Sweet & Maxwell – Sweet & Maxwell are the publishers of the *Current Legal Information* CD-ROM, which contains *Current Law* from 1986, Legal Journals Index, Daily Law Reports, Financial Journals Index, Badger (a database of supplementary legal materials), and the Inns of Court Catalogues. They also publish the *White Book Service* (formerly the *Supreme Court Practice*), *Archbold: Criminal Pleading, Evidence and Practice* and many CD-ROMs which contain precedents, such as *Practical Commercial Precedents*, *Practical Lease Precedents*, and *Practical Trust Precedents*.

Jordans – publishers of a range of electronic reference materials, including *Civil Court Service* on CD-ROM and, under their Family Law imprint, the Fam Lex Library CD-ROM.

Other materials which are available on CD-ROM and are of interest to lawyers include *Hansard*, *The Times* and *Financial Times*.

7.2.2 Using CD-ROMs

Unfortunately, different producers of CD-ROMs have produced different software. The search commands used on JUSTIS products, for example, will be different to those used on *The Times*.

However, CD-ROMs are designed to be 'user-friendly' and all have built-in Help buttons, if not tutorials, and the majority follow the same basic principles for searching as outlined above.

7.3 INTRODUCTION TO ON-LINE MATERIALS

7.3.1 What is available on-line?

Most of the material available on CD-ROM (including most of that mentioned in **7.2.1**) is also available on-line. Much additional material is available (in electronic form) only on-line. The situation is changing daily and there is often a wide choice of sources for the same material. The following can serve only as examples.

7.3.2 LEXIS

LEXIS is one of the largest and most well known of the legal databases. Originally developed in the USA, it consequently has large 'libraries' of American law. However, the UK and EU libraries are extensive, with much useful up-to-date information. These are full-text primary sources, such as case reports, statutes and statutory instruments. Legal journals and a vast array of other useful sources from around the world are also available.

7.3.3 Westlaw-UK

Westlaw is another enormous database, originally for American law. Westlaw-UK (provided by Sweet & Maxwell) has vast quantities of UK, EU and other material. It contains many series of law reports (including *The Law Reports*, *Common Market Law Reports*, *European Human Rights Reports* and *Lloyd's Law Reports*), a number of legal journals, legal directories and sources of company information. It also contains a vast range of newspapers and magazines.

7.3.4 Butterworths Direct

This source provides electronic versions of *Halsbury's Laws*, *Statutes* and *Statutory Instruments*. It also has the *All England Law Reports*, a legal news service and much more besides.

7.3.5 LAWTEL

LAWTEL is an on-line legal database which is updated on a daily basis. To access LAWTEL, you have to pay an annual subscription.

It contains summaries of cases, personal injury reports, and practice directions from 1980; statutory instruments and statutes in summary format from 1984, but with full text from 1997 and 1996 respectively; details of commencement orders and repeals from 1986; the progress of Bills through Parliament, including where to obtain copies of White Papers and Green Papers; an articles index going back to 1994; and *The Lawyer* in full text from August 1994 and *The Legal Executive* in full text from 1996.

LAWTEL users can also access summaries of European information on the Spicers database, the Waterlows Directory of Solicitors and the Havers Directory of Barristers.

7.3.6 Some other Internet sources

The list is endless. Government departments (eg the DTI, the Treasury, the Home Office, the Inland Revenue and the Lord Chancellor's Department) have their own useful sites, as do Parliament and the EU institutions. Hansard is available electronically.

Chapter 8

THE RESULTS OF LEGAL RESEARCH

8.1 INTRODUCTION

Chapters 3 to 7 have described some of the sources which may be available to you when you are asked to look up a point of law. This chapter offers some advice about how the research should actually be done.

8.2 RECORDING RESEARCH

You may be tempted, when researching a problem, not to make any notes at all and rely on memory when giving an oral or a written report. In many cases, a quick answer is all that is wanted. But what if your principal questions the answer, or wants you to check back on something, or asks you how you have gone about the research?

It is good practice to jot down notes as you research. It will be helpful to note sources used, keywords checked, and page and other references for sources found. It is important to check, as a matter of routine, the date of the source, the 'law stated' date for a textbook, or the date of the latest issue for a looseleaf or electronic work. Making a note helps to form the habit. Brief notes should also be made of the content of relevant sources. The resulting notes may make sense only to you, but should be capable of forming the basis of a report.

8.3 REPORTING

If you are researching on behalf of your principal, it is important that you communicate the results clearly. In any event, it is as well to make a clear record of the legal basis for advice. Obviously, the nature of the record will vary with the research – in particular whether the researcher knows the full background to the client's problem – but the following points should be borne in mind.

(1) The main aims of the report should be to provide a clear answer to the question posed, and to give enough detail of the research for the answer to be easily checked, and relevant sources traced.
(2) It is a good idea to restate the problem researched. If you have a different view of the problem from your principal, you are unlikely to produce a satisfactory answer. It may be necessary to remind your principal of the problem. If it is a complex problem involving several issues, you should list the issues and research and report on each one separately.
(3) The report should state the date when it was completed.
(4) It will be helpful to give a clear answer to the problem, separately from any reasoning or source references, so that the main message is quickly apparent.
(5) The report should contain source references. These should include the correct title and citation of relevant primary sources, and page or paragraph numbers for

Chapter 8 contents
Introduction
Recording research
Reporting

the works where they were found, or considered. If necessary, a photocopy of relevant material (or print-out from an electronic source) can be attached.

(6) It is important to state what steps have been taken to update, and to give the date of the latest sources used including the commencement dates of statutes and statutory instruments.

(7) The results can be presented in note form, using technical language if appropriate, and assuming knowledge of the legal background.

(8) If the factual context is known, the results should be applied to the facts, and brief notes made of obvious practical implications.

Of course, reports in practice may take different forms, depending on their purpose and importance, The assumption made throughout this section has been that you will begin with relatively simple tasks, so that a simple form of report will suffice. In the Drafting section of this Resource Book (**1.4.1**), you will find suggestions for the content of more elaborate forms of report, together with useful advice on style and layout.

PART III

ORAL COMMUNICATION SKILLS

Chapter 9

INTRODUCTION TO ORAL COMMUNICATION SKILLS

9.1 GENERAL

Chapter 9 contents
General
Listening
Questioning
Non-verbal communication

> 'One-third of what is said is not heard
> One-third is heard but not understood
> One-third is understood – but may not be accepted'
> (adapted from a passage in *The Skills of Negotiating* by Bill Scott)

All solicitors need to possess good oral communication skills in order to defeat the 'one-third rule' (above) and to become effective interviewers (Chapter 10), negotiators (Chapter 11) or advocates (Chapter 12).

Solicitors also need to establish and maintain good working relationships with their colleagues in the office (whether professional or administrative), with members of other professions whom they have to consult or instruct, and with representatives of official bodies (eg court staff).

Although oral communication skills are largely based on common sense, people's ability to use them varies enormously. Some people are naturally better than others, but everyone is capable of improvement. Like any other skill (driving a car, playing a musical instrument, playing a sport), performance can be improved by learning specific skills and techniques, and then practising them.

At first, practising new techniques can feel artificial ('It's just not me') but after a while the technique usually becomes second nature (like changing gear in a car). However, skills training should not be allowed to suppress natural ability, and it is possible to be a competent interviewer, negotiator or advocate without necessarily having to perform every technique by the book. It is a question of balance; but success comes through practising sound techniques. Brilliant mavericks are rare.

This chapter introduces those aspects of oral communication skills which are common to interviewing, negotiation and advocacy. Chapters 10–12 explain how the skills apply to each of these activities.

9.2 LISTENING

In order to advise a client, or to persuade an opponent or the court, solicitors have first to *demonstrate* that they have both heard and understood what the other has said.

This involves listening carefully to what is being said. However, listening is an underrated skill which requires considerable concentration. Listening as a solicitor is very different from listening in the context of ordinary social discourse, where interchanges are shorter and more fluid and where there is less need to pick up every nuance or recall precisely what was said. Listening as a solicitor is also different from listening to lectures, where students do not necessarily have to interrelate with the lecturer and may be able to copy up notes from elsewhere later. Nevertheless, students who are good listeners in lectures will find that this skill will help them enormously in practice.

Most authorities on oral communication skills make a distinction between 'passive listening' and 'active listening'.

9.2.1 Passive listening

Passive listening involves using silences and other unobtrusive signals to encourage the speaker to continue. For example, when interviewing, negotiating or conducting advocacy, the solicitor might want to induce the speaker to carry on speaking and thereby perhaps volunteer a crucial piece of information.

Silences can be embarrassing in normal social situations, so many people learn during their upbringing to avoid them. Yet silence is one of the most powerful techniques available to a solicitor. It may require a conscious effort to remain silent for longer than normal in the hope that the speaker will fill the void with more information.

Other non-obtrusive signals a solicitor may give the speaker to encourage him to continue include:

- eye contact;
- posture;
- nodding;
- acknowledgments ('Uh, huh');
- express invitations ('Go on').

9.2.2 Active listening

Active listening, as the phrase suggests, involves more obtrusive techniques which demonstrate to the other person that the solicitor has both heard and understood.

The most common form of active listening is summarising, ie giving a short, clear precis of what the speaker has just said. Like silence, the technique is not regularly employed in social conversations and so requires a conscious effort.

Summarising is also used by solicitors to check the effectiveness of communication in the reverse direction, ie that the other person has heard and understood the solicitor.

9.3 QUESTIONING

Questioning skills are well-known tools of the solicitor's trade. Questions can be classified according to the breadth of the response they allow, ie as open or closed questions.

9.3.1 Open questions

Open questions give maximum freedom to the person being questioned, they encourage expansion, and they do not seek to influence the content of the reply.

Examples
'So what happened next?'
'What were your reactions to that?'
'How did you respond to the offer?'
'Why did you do that?'
'Tell me about your relationship with the managing director.'
'Tell me more about ...'

Open questions do not necessarily have to be worded as questions: 'Tell me ...' is a phrase which can be used to invite an open response.

9.3.2 Closed questions

Closed questions invite a narrow answer, from a few words or a sentence to a 'Yes'/'No' reply (sometimes called 'Yes/No questions').

Examples
'Were you also carrying a knife?'
'Did you accept the offer?'

One particular form of closed question is the leading question. For example, the questioner might deliberately seek to influence the content of the reply by asking a question which encourages a particular answer 'So you must have been drunk, mustn't you?'

9.4 NON-VERBAL COMMUNICATION

Non-verbal communication includes eye contact, posture and gestures and is often called 'body language'.

Careful observation of the body language of other people can provide clues as to how they are feeling, or how they are responding to advice or to an argument, and can therefore be influential in deciding how to proceed. However, tread cautiously, because the clue might not be conclusive: the interpretation of body language is controversial, and is subject to cultural variations. Be aware of non-verbal communication, but do not allow it to distract you from everything else.

Similarly, awareness of how your own body language affects both yourself and others can help in deciding how to convey your message more effectively. Although it is sometimes said that one cannot (or should not) 'fake' body language, cause and effect are often interrelated. Sitting with your arms tightly folded and your legs crossed, or nervously drumming your fingers or tapping your foot, can affect your own feelings as well as influencing others' perceptions of you. Sitting or standing in a physically relaxed manner can help you feel more relaxed.

A useful book is *Body Language* by Alan Pease (Sheldon Press).

Chapter 10

INTERVIEWING AND ADVISING

10.1 OBJECTIVES OF A SOLICITOR/CLIENT INTERVIEW

This chapter concentrates on the skills needed during the first interview with a client. There are four main objectives:

(1) to establish good **rapport** between the solicitor and the client;
(2) to obtain relevant **information** from the client;
(3) to help the client reach appropriate **decisions**;
(4) to plan future **action**.

Other legal interviews (eg with witnesses) usually serve more limited purposes.

10.2 COMMON FAILINGS

There are many reasons why a solicitor may fail to achieve the above objectives. For example, the solicitor may:

- fail to listen properly;
- talk too much;
- make a premature diagnosis;
- restrict the areas in which the client feels free to talk;
- be over-directive in suggesting what further action is necessary.

The skills referred to later in this chapter will reduce the likelihood of any of these failings occuring.

10.3 TWO INGREDIENTS FOR SUCCESS – SKILLS AND STRUCTURE

10.3.1 Skills

In order to achieve the objectives referred to in **10.1**, a solicitor needs to make effective use of a wide range of skills.

The principal skills involved are:

(1) **listening**
(2) **questioning**
(3) **analysing**
(4) **explaining**
(5) **note-taking.**

These will be considered in more detail in **10.4**.

Chapter 10 contents
Objectives of a solicitor/client interview
Common failings
Two ingredients for success – skills and structure
The skills
Structure and management
Further reading

10.3.2 Structure

The objectives in **10.1** are easier to achieve if the solicitor prepares for and conducts the interview in a logical and coherent manner.

Structure and management involve:

(1) creating a **suitable environment** for the interview;
(2) **preparing adequately** for the interview;
(3) using an **appropriate 'model'** for the interview itself.

A 'model' is merely a predetermined structure, under which the interview is divided into a logical sequence of stages. Each stage involves the performance of essential tasks and requires the use of different combinations of the skills referred to above.

The model used in this book is:

GREETING
―――――――
(1) PRELIMINARIES
(2) OBTAINING THE FACTS
(3) FILLING IN THE DETAIL
(4) ADVISING
(5) CLOSING
―――――――
PARTING

The model is easy to follow and can be used in any legal context, although the length of time spent on each stage will usually vary depending on whether the interview is litigation or transaction based.

A detailed explanation of these stages will be given at **10.5** but a brief overview of the three central stages will help your understanding of what follows in **10.4** about the relevant skills. Thus:

Obtaining the facts

Involves the client giving an account of the matter with as little interruption from the solicitor as possible. It is therefore characterised by the client talking and the solicitor **listening** and encouraging the client to continue.

Filling in the detail

Involves a more active role by the solicitor to ensure that a complete and accurate picture is obtained and recorded. This stage is therefore characterised by the solicitor **questioning** the client and taking notes of what the client says.

Advising

Involves supplying the information which the client needs in order to make necessary decisions and to give the solicitor instructions for any further action. This stage therefore usually takes the form of the solicitor analysing and **explaining** the client's position, explaining the range of options open to the client and then **engaging in a dialogue** to make necessary decisions and to agree a plan of action.

10.4 THE SKILLS

10.4.1 Listening – an undervalued skill

Encouraging a client to tell his/her own story is generally a more effective way of gathering information than attempting to do so by a series of closed questions. You should therefore avoid asking questions until you have a reasonably full version of the case.

If the client is verbose, you may need to adopt a more forceful braking role, but this should occur only when absolutely necessary.

Listening is an undervalued skill which involves a range of techniques to sustain information-giving.

Silence

In everyday conversation, periods of silence can sometimes seem awkward and even cause embarrassment.

In an interview, these periods give the client time to think, tell the story as he/she remembers it, and express the feelings it creates.

You must therefore learn to control the natural urge to fill silences.

Body language

Consider how your body language may help or hinder building good rapport with the client. For example:

(1) eye contact: a friendly, but not a prolonged stare;
(2) posture: leaning slightly towards the client;
(3) head-nodding: but not too much;
(4) avoiding irritating/distracting mannerisms, eg pen-tapping, foot-drumming, etc.

Acknowledgments

Brief indications (without interrupting) showing attention, interest, and understanding, such as:

'Yes, I see'

'... in Brussels?'

'Mhmmmm'.

Invitations to continue/elaborate

Examples are:

'Go on'

'What happened?'

'Tell me more about that'.

Reflecting feeling

This involves making it clear that you understand how the client feels; for example: 'I can quite see why you feel so angry about this' or (in relation to bereavement) 'I'm sorry to hear that'.

It involves expressing empathy with the client's feelings; not being judgmental about them.

The technique is useful in building rapport and is particularly important where the client's emotions will be a major factor in the case, for example in matrimonial cases or where the client has recently been bereaved.

However, reflecting feeling may also be appropriate in interviews which may appear to be less personal, for example when a commercial client has anxieties about losing face within the company if a transaction fails to reach a satisfactory conclusion.

You can gain valuable insights into the client's feelings by observing and correctly interpreting the client's body language, not merely from listening to the client's words and tone of voice.

10.4.2 Questioning

In an initial interview, a solicitor needs to obtain information on:

(1) the nature of the client's problem or proposed transaction;
(2) the relevant background facts;
(3) the client's feelings and objectives.

Whilst much of this may be obtained through use of the listening techniques discussed above, it will usually be necessary to clarify and probe further by questioning.

For an initial interview, particularly in the early stages, open questions usually have more advantages than closed questions and failure to recognise this leads many interviews into an interviewer-dominated style.

(1) Open questions

The advantages of open questions are that they:

- allow the client to select the subject-matter;
- allow the client to select the information the client believes to be relevant;
- allow the client to start with information about which the client feels comfortable;
- enable the client to get things 'off his chest';
- give the client freedom to reflect and to feel more actively involved in the interview;
- encourage memory by association, which may produce information which would be overlooked if the client were asked only closed questions.

The disadvantages are that they:

- may initially produce insufficient information;
- may encourage the client to verbosity and/or irrelevance;
- may inhibit a reticent client.

(2) Closed questions

The advantages of closed questions are that they:

- are a good method of obtaining precise details;
- may guide a client less stressfully through a sensitive area;
- may give confidence to an initially reticent or anxious client;

- may help to prompt memory;
- help to clarify and probe areas of ambiguity or uncertainty;
- may quieten a verbose client.

The disadvantages are that they:

- may lead to an over-clinical or 'processing' style of interview;
- may deprive the client of the opportunity to state the case in his own words;
- may inhibit rapport;
- reduce the opportunity to listen to and observe the client, and to understand his needs;
- may lead the solicitor to miss important areas of information because the client is not allowed to associate ideas freely;
- may even result in the solicitor's directing the interview down a totally irrelevant path.

(3) The 'T-funnel'

The use of open questions followed by closed questions is sometimes known as the T-funnel sequence of questioning:

```
┌─────────────────┐
│  OPEN QUESTIONS │
└─────┬─────┬─────┘
      │     │
   ┌──┴─────┴──┐
   │  CLOSED   │
   │ QUESTIONS │
   └───────────┘
```

The solicitor introduces a particular topic with a series of open questions. Only after the open questions cease to be productive should they be narrowed into closed questions.

Premature use of closed questions may distort the response or lead to important details being omitted.

Example

(Open questions)

Solicitor	'What happened next?'
Client	'I got out of my car.'
Solicitor	'Yes ...?'
Client	'Well, I went over to where he'd parked his car and spoke to him.'

(Closed questions)

Solicitor	'Could you tell me exactly where you were both standing and exactly what was said?'
Client	'Yes, he was standing by the offside front wing of his car and as I approached him I am afraid I told him what I thought of him.'
Solicitor	'Can you remember the words you actually used?'
Client	'I said "You're a ***** – why the hell didn't you indicate?"'
Solicitor	'Did he reply?'

Client	'Yes, he said "I'm sorry – I didn't realise they'd changed the lane markings."'
Solicitor	'Anything else?'
Client	'No.'
Solicitor	'Was anyone else present?'
Client	'Yes – his wife was standing right next to him.'

(4) Further clarification and probing

It will often be necessary to probe further:

- to resolve remaining areas of ambiguity;
- to jog the client's memory;
- to clarify client needs and reaction to consequences of action;
- to discover how the client will respond to the legal process (in litigation) or to a counter-argument or proposal (negotiating a transaction).

The following are some techniques to achieve these objectives.

GOING BACK ONE STAGE

This involves taking the client back one stage in the narrative and inviting the client to relive the sequence of events in order to jog the memory:

'Take me through that again but starting from before you were approaching the road junction.'

This is a useful technique but there is a danger that the client may fill any gaps in the narrative by supplying facts which are incorrect but which the client (often quite sincerely) believes must inevitably have occurred.

LEADING QUESTIONS

Leading questions can be a useful way of helping clients to convey something which they may have difficulty in articulating in their own words:

'So you've had disagreements with the managing director before?'

'So sexual intercourse did take place on that occasion?'

PREFACING A QUESTION WITH EXPLANATION

This can counteract the client perceiving your question as irrelevant or allay the client's anxiety in a sensitive area. For example:

'I know you're very confident of being acquitted but, if you are convicted, the magistrates will sentence you immediately. For that reason I now need to ask you some questions about your financial circumstances.'

There is, however, a danger that the explanation may influence (and therefore distort) the client's reply.

CROSS-CHECKING

This is often necessary where the information given by the client reveals gaps or contradictions which require explanation. For example:

'Are you quite sure about that because according to the police report you said you'd drunk 3 pints?'

DEVIL'S ADVOCATE

To play devil's advocate is to suggest to the client a different and adverse interpretation of his story. For example:

> 'If you're so sure that the accident wasn't your fault, why did you say to the other motorist: "I'm sorry – I just didn't see you coming"?'

It is generally advisable to explain why you are doing this because, otherwise, your apparent hostility is likely to damage rapport. For example:

> 'I'm sorry to ask you so bluntly but it's a question you are bound to be asked in court if this gets to trial.'

CHECKLISTS

Some interviews lend themselves to the use of checklists.

Used appropriately, a checklist has the obvious advantage that essential information is unlikely to be overlooked. A checklist also provides you with a concise and convenient source of information for speedy future reference.

However, interviewing a client simply by running through a checklist, particularly at the beginning of the interview, may inhibit effective communication. You may appear to be merely 'processing a case' rather than listening to the client's unique personal problem.

Indeed, premature use of a checklist (ie before a correct diagnosis of the problem has been made) can waste valuable time while a mass of irrelevant information is accumulated. In other words, make quite sure that your chosen checklist is appropriate before using it!

(5) *Summarising*

This is an extremely important and useful technique.

Its purpose is to double check that your understanding of the facts and of your client's feelings is correct.

A summary of the key facts should be given at the end of the filling in the detail stage and before moving into the advising stage:

> 'OK, now before we talk about what needs to be done let me just check with you that I have got a correct and complete list of all your relevant assets.'

Apart from giving the client an opportunity to correct errors and supply additional facts, summarising reassures the client that you have heard and understood what you have been told. It also gives you a useful breathing space to think about the matter and the advice that needs to be given. It may also identify some areas on which further questioning is needed before you can safely advise.

Remember that summarising your understanding of the client's feelings and objectives is just as important as summarising factual information.

> 'So let me see whether I've correctly understood what you are hoping to achieve out of all this ...'

> 'So would it be fair to say that you would only be prepared to go to court if Janice's name could be kept out of it?'

Summarising helps you to identify when further questions need to be asked and what advice to give.

10.4.3 Analysing

Once the facts and the client's goals have been identified, the solicitor must (at least mentally) analyse which facts and legal principles are relevant, how the law applies to those facts and so reach a conclusion about the client's position and the range of available courses of action.

This process is familiar even to an inexperienced solicitor because it involves essentially the same techniques needed to answer traditional problem-solving questions in law examinations.

One obvious difference is that in real life the solicitor has to elicit the relevant information rather than having it spoon-fed in the form of a given scenario. Another difference is that the solicitor has little or no time for quiet reflection before being expected to offer at least a tentative view of the position.

What tends to happen in most interviews is that, at quite an early stage, the solicitor starts to form a provisional theory about the likely end position. This inevitably has to be reviewed and modified as additional information emerges and the solicitor must be careful to avoid reaching a conclusion until all the facts have been obtained.

Like all skills, this process becomes easier with experience, practice and greater familiarity with the law in question.

Listening, questioning, note-taking and trying to formulate advice cannot be tackled simultaneously – just one reason why it is helpful to build in periods of 'thinking time' as discussed in **10.4.2***(5)* above.

10.4.4 Explaining

Once you have analysed the client's position, a number of matters will usually have to be explained before the client can be expected to make decisions and give instructions.

This frequently involves explaining concepts which will be second nature to you and which you would normally express in legal terminology (such as 'consideration' or 'implied conditions/warranties' etc).

It is therefore easy to overlook the simple fact that concepts and terminology which seem quite straightforward and normal to you can be totally bewildering and meaningless to a lay client.

Clarity is vital and legal jargon should therefore be avoided at all costs. You must bear constantly in mind that **accurate and faultlessly reasoned advice is utterly useless to a client who cannot understand it**.

You should also bear in mind that, even when you have explained matters clearly, it is often unrealistic to expect the client to remember everything once the interview is over. For this reason it is desirable in most cases to send a follow-up letter to the client summarising the advice which you have given.

It is often helpful to ask the client whether what you have said has been understood and offer to repeat the advice. If overdone, this technique may appear patronising. If used appropriately, even the most self-confident client will appreciate your concern and a more timid client, who may be reluctant to ask directly, will welcome a genuine offer of clarification.

10.4.5 Note-taking

Note-taking is an important and difficult skill.

No solicitor can memorise every piece of information on all his/her files and there may be occasions when some other member of the firm will need to take over the file permanently or temporarily.

The file must therefore contain a complete, accurate and legible record of the interview.

This is best achieved by taking manuscript notes during the interview itself and, if necessary, having a fuller and/or clearer version typed afterwards.

Failing to take notes during the interview and intending to dictate everything immediately after the interview is fraught with danger because you may unavoidably become involved in other distractions and be unable to do this before memory has faded. The longhand notes must, at minimum, be sufficient to operate as an aide memoire of the vital facts, dates, assets, etc from which a fuller record can later be prepared.

Difficulties can arise if you try to take detailed notes too early in the interview, while the client is trying to tell his/her story. If you write while the client is actually talking, this can damage rapport for two reasons. First, it is very difficult to follow the meaning of what the client is saying if you are frantically trying to translate it into a written note. Secondly, it is impossible to write at length without losing eye contact with the client. Few things are more off-putting for a client than trying to relate a story to the top of someone's head! On the other hand, it can be equally off-putting if you interrupt the flow of the client's narrative by requesting time to write everything down.

The solution is simple. **Do not attempt to take notes during the obtaining the facts stage**; instead, concentrate on listening to the client's version of events and defer taking notes until the 'filling in the detail' stage. This may mean that you have to ask the client to repeat some matters but is likely to be less time consuming in the long run. Alternatively, restrict note-taking to very brief jottings which do not destroy eye contact but which will serve at a later stage as reminders of topics which need to be expanded.

Even when fuller note-taking starts, try to develop a concise style and be selective about what you write down. Headings can be used effectively to give a structure to your notes. Ensure that key names, addresses, figures, dates and verbatim accounts of conversations are accurately worded. Never be embarrassed to ask the client for the correct spellings if names are unfamiliar.

10.5 STRUCTURE AND MANAGEMENT

10.5.1 Before the interview

The environment

It is important that the interview should take place in an environment which will help rather than hinder effective communication. The aim should be to create an atmosphere in which the client will feel calm and relaxed and which will give a favourable impression of you and your firm.

You should therefore ensure:

(1) that the client will be physically comfortable;
(2) that the interview will be free from unnecessary interruptions;
(3) that the office surroundings convey a sense of well-organised professionalism without being austere and/or impersonal.

Seating arrangements may also help or hinder effective communication. Views on this topic differ and an arrangement which seems friendly and welcoming to one client may strike another as over-familiar or even invasive.

However, as far as possible, the arrangement should be one in which:

(1) the solicitor and client can clearly see and hear each other;
(2) the client does not feel kept at a distance at one extreme or invaded at the other;
(3) the solicitor and (if necessary) the client can make written notes in comfort.

The traditional arrangement in which the solicitor and client face each other from opposite sides of the solicitor's desk will usually satisfy the above criteria, provided the desk is not piled high with files and papers. It is also the arrangement which most clients will be expecting.

However, depending on the personality of the client and the nature of the matter, you may decide that a less formal arrangement, perhaps without the intervening desk, would be more relaxing for the client and therefore more conducive to communication.

Furthermore, there may be occasions (eg where the client needs to explain a plan, diagram or map to the solicitor) when sitting alongside the client is the only effective arrangement.

You should therefore consider the possibility of other arrangements and adopt them whenever appropriate.

The above comments presuppose that the interview will take place in an environment over which you have some degree of control, but the interview may, for a variety of reasons, take place in surroundings (eg hospital ward, prison cell, crowded court corridor, etc) over which you will have little or no control.

Preparing for the interview

Where possible/appropriate, you should:

(1) obtain background information on the client (and the client's business);
(2) request relevant documents and consider them in advance;
(3) research the relevant area of law, being careful not to pre-judge the issues or 'pigeon-hole' the client;
(4) make a checklist;

(5) ensure that the interview will be free from interruptions (especially the telephone).

10.5.2 The model

<u>GREETING</u>

    (1)   PRELIMINARIES
    (2)   OBTAINING THE FACTS
    (3)   FILLING IN THE DETAIL
    (4)   ADVISING
    (5)   <u>CLOSING</u>

PARTING

What now follows is a step-by-step account of each successive stage in the model, indicating the purpose of each stage and which skills need to be employed.

10.5.3 Greeting

The importance of a warm and friendly greeting cannot be over-emphasised.

When you are ready to see the client, either go yourself to the reception area and escort the client to where the interview will take place, or make sure that some other member of staff does so. A client who is left to find his/her own way to your office through a bewildering maze of corridors is unlikely to arrive feeling welcome.

The client will form an impression of you immediately you meet. You should therefore do everything possible to ensure that this impression is favourable and that the client is made to feel welcome, comfortable and relaxed.

Greet the client by shaking hands, making eye contact and addressing the client by name. You should also introduce yourself by name and explain your status within the firm (eg trainee solicitor, solicitor, partner, etc).

The above points are simply common courtesy and may seem obvious, but they are extremely important.

After greeting, it is a matter of judgement how quickly you proceed to the business at hand, but most clients will have been rehearsing what they wish to say and will be ready to begin at once.

10.5.4 Preliminaries

In most cases, the client will have given some indication of the general nature of the problem and the reason for seeking advice when arranging the appointment for the interview.

Indeed, it is important to train secretaries and administrative staff who arrange appointments to make suitable enquiries to ensure that the client sees a solicitor whose expertise is appropriate to the matter in question.

Nevertheless, ambiguities may still arise. 'I want to see a solicitor about a will' may not necessarily mean that the client wishes to make a will. It is therefore sensible to **ask the client to confirm your understanding of the reason for the visit before encouraging the client to launch into a lengthy account of the facts.**

Once this confirmation has been obtained there are two matters which should be dealt with before the interview proceeds further.

(1) How is the interview to be paid for?

Clients naturally tend to be concerned about the cost of the interview and, indeed, of the job itself. Until the complete picture has been obtained, it is usually difficult to say anything meaningful about the latter and this must therefore be postponed until the closing stages of the interview.

However, as far as the cost of the interview itself is concerned, now is a good time to ascertain whether the matter and the client are covered by some form of legal aid.

Alternatively, explain to the client what your charging rate is or, if such be the case, that the firm's policy is to charge a fixed fee, for example for an initial half-hour interview. Once this has been explained clearly to the client, you should check whether the client is genuinely content to accept this arrangement.

(2) How will the interview be conducted?

It makes sense to start by letting the client know how long you have available for the interview and to find out whether the client is under any time constraints.

It is also helpful to say a little about how you propose to conduct the interview:

> 'In a minute I'll ask you to give me the background information. Then I will probably need to ask you some questions and make some notes. Finally, when I have got the complete picture, I shall explain what your legal position is and what options I think are open to you. Between us, we can then try to decide which course of action would best suit your needs.'

Skills summary
(1) Listening
(2) Open questions
(3) No (or very brief) note-taking.

10.5.5 Obtaining the facts

The objective is to obtain the client's account of the facts or of the proposed transaction.

This objective should be achieved by encouraging the client to give an account of the matter in his or her own words with as little interruption from you as possible.

Consider the impact on the client of the following choice of words and expressions:

> 'So, where shall we start?' (Doesn't inspire confidence)

> 'What's the problem, then?' (There may not be a 'problem')

> 'Thank you for sending me the documentation ... It seems to me ...' (Over directional – premature diagnosis)

> 'Things don't look too good, do they?' (Prematurely pessimistic – provokes anxiety)

> 'Don't worry, we'll sort this out for you.' (Prematurely optimistic – raises expectations)

'Funny, this is the sixth one we've had in like this in the last month.' (Treating client as a 'case' to be processed – not a human being)

'This is the one, I think. Now then, where are we? ... Let me see ... dah dah dah dah ... Oh yes that's right, this is a GBH case, isn't it?' (Disorganised – unprepared – confusing use of jargon)

Clearly, therefore, you must give very careful thought to the form of words which you use to invite the client to begin this process.

If you are interviewing a client about a road accident it may be perfectly sensible to say 'Perhaps you could start by telling me exactly what happened on the day in question'.

On the other hand, if the client wishes to make a will, saying 'Could you now give me some general background information?' or 'Just tell me the story in your own words' is too vague to indicate what sort of information you require. A more focused wording would be 'Perhaps you could start by giving me a brief summary of everything which you own and a general idea of who you are thinking of leaving it to'.

Whatever form of opening words you decide upon, it can also be helpful if, during this part of the interview, you also ask a question along the lines of 'It would also be helpful if you could let me know any particular concerns which you have or problems which you foresee'.

You should concentrate on using the various listening techniques discussed in **10.4.1** and confine questions to open questions which will encourage the client to continue the narrative.

There will be ample opportunity in the next stage of the interview ('Filling in the detail') to clarify matters. You should therefore resist any temptation to do so at this stage, because a series of closed questions can easily destroy the client's concentration.

For the same reason, making written notes should, if possible, be restricted to what can be written without interrupting the client's narrative flow (see **10.4.5**).

This comparatively passive role can be a difficult one to master if you are a naturally talkative person. It does, however, enable you to maintain eye contact with the client and to observe the client's general demeanour and manner of delivery. This is very helpful in building rapport with the client and in picking up body language signals about the client's feelings.

Skills summary
(1) Listening
(2) Open questions
(3) Brief note-taking.

10.5.6 Filling in the detail

The objective is to ensure that you obtain a full and accurate understanding and record of the relevant facts and of the client's wishes and objectives.

You will not usually be able to give the client effective advice immediately after the client has completed his or her account of the matter in the 'Obtaining the facts' stage.

In most cases, it will be necessary to ask the client to fill gaps or explain discrepancies in the narrative or to supply information which the client had not considered to be relevant.

You will also need to take written notes and check that you have correctly understood what the client has said. It may also be necessary to examine documents.

This is the stage of the interview during which you assume a more active and directive role.

Questioning skills become more important although, even at this stage, it is generally best to use the T-funnel approach (discussed in **10.4.2**). In other words, see what information can be elicited in response to open questions before pinning down the client with more specific closed questions.

This is the stage when it may be necessary to use some of the clarifying and probing techniques (see **10.4.2(4)**) to jog the client's memory or to explore discrepancies or weaknesses in the client's version of events.

Before completing this stage of the interview and moving on to give advice, it is important to summarise what the client has said in order to double check that you have correctly understood the position (see **10.4.2(5)**).

Skills summary
(1) Questioning – the T-funnel approach
(2) Note-taking
(3) Clarifying and probing
(4) Examining documents
(5) Summarising.

10.5.7 Advising

The solicitor:

(1) explains the legal position of the client;
(2) discusses with the client the main options (both legal and non-legal);
(3) helps the client to reach a decision/give instructions;
(4) agrees a plan of action.

Explaining the client's legal position

The client's legal position should be explained in simple and comprehensible language. You should therefore avoid jargon. Furthermore, you should be aware that the amount of information which a client can absorb is limited (see **10.4.4**).

This is the first interview. Therefore, if:

(1) the matter is not routine; or
(2) you do not have experience in the particular area of law; or
(3) the client does not insist on preliminary 'off the cuff' advice; or
(4) the matter is not urgent,

it is quite proper to postpone advising until you have had an opportunity to carry out research.

Clients do not always need or expect to be given immediate advice.

Discussing the main options

The client is generally less interested in being given a detailed resumé of the law than in being told what courses of action are available. You should therefore identify all possible options and discuss the relative merits of each option thoroughly with the client. This will usually involve discussing the financial cost of each option but should also take account of such non-legal factors as, for example, the emotional stress of continuing litigation.

You should try to involve the client in the discussion so that you can jointly weigh the advantages and disadvantages of each option.

Helping the client to reach a decision

All major decisions concerning the case or transaction are for the client to make. It is the client's case, not the solicitor's. However, opinion is divided on how far the solicitor may recommend a course of action for the client.

There are two schools of thought.

(1) The non-directive school suggests that a solicitor should only present the options and leave it entirely to the client to decide which to follow. The advice is characterised by the preamble, 'On the one hand X, but on the other hand Y. However, it is for you to decide'.

This approach may avoid a charge of negligence if the route followed by the client proves to be the wrong option. However, it is not particularly helpful to the client. Given the status, experience and cost of solicitors, clients often expect a recommendation.

(2) The directive school involves the solicitor in taking greater control of the decision-making process.

A combination of each approach is appropriate in most cases. It is important to explain the realistic options to the client and to explore the positive and negative consequences of each. Provided the client actively participates in this explorative discussion and you actively seek the client's views and preferences, the decision will often be clear.

Furthermore, if the matter is non-urgent, difficult or complex, the client may need time to reach a considered decision.

Agreeing a future plan of action

Once key decisions have been taken, it will usually be necessary to agree a more detailed plan of campaign, ie to decide what is the best way of carrying out the course of action which has been agreed.

For example, if your client has decided to try to settle a matter by agreement rather than go to court, you will still need to decide:

- whether to approach the other side immediately or await their next move;
- whether any first approach should be made by you or the client, and if so:

(i) whether it should be by letter, telephone or in person;

(ii) what (if any) opening offer should be made and how far the client is prepared to go in order to settle.

As before, you should clearly explain the range of options and try to engage the client as fully as possible in the decision-making process.

Skills summary
(1) Summarising
(2) Explaining
(3) Note-taking.

10.5.8 Closing

Once the issues have been discussed with the client and the client has decided what needs to be done, there are still a number of matters to deal with before you conclude the interview.

You should always make sure that the client has had an opportunity to discuss all matters and concerns and that The Law Society's recommendations on client care have been followed.

As far as the former is concerned, make a specific point of asking the client 'Is there anything else that you want to talk about before we finish and is there anything which we've discussed which you would like me to clarify?' This should not be treated as a meaningless ritual, and the client should be made to feel free to respond affirmatively.

Other matters of client care are contained in Rule 15 of the Solicitors' Practice Rules 1990 and are set out in the Appendix to Part II of the LPC Resource Book *Pervasive and Core Topics* (Jordans). Paragraph **10.7.1** of the *Pervasive and Core Topics* book sets out the following commentary:

> 'At a first interview, The Law Society recommends that a client should be informed of:
>
> (1) the name and status of the person who will be handling the case and the name of another person in the firm whom the client may contact (particularly if a problem arises);
>
> (2) what action the solicitor will be taking on the client's behalf, including the next immediate step in the case or transaction;
>
> (3) what action (if any) the client has to take;
>
> (4) the likely duration of the matter, including the approximate time when the solicitor will next contact the client;
>
> (5) the likely cost of the matter and how this cost will be funded, whether privately, by legal aid or by legal expenses insurance.'

Dealing with the points in the above order:

(1) Name and status of person handling the case

Giving the name and status of the person who will be handling the case is something which will probably have been explained as part of the greeting or preliminaries stage of the interview. Giving the name of another person in the firm as an alternative point of contact can appropriately be dealt with as part of the closing stage of the interview. Details of any complaints procedure is something which could also be dealt with at this stage, but in practice is more commonly included in a follow-up letter written to the client after the interview.

(2) Follow-up tasks by solicitor

It is clearly helpful to summarise what steps you have agreed to take and when you will take them. The steps will vary from case to case but might involve taking a statement from a witness, obtaining a police or medical report, writing a letter before action, preparing a draft will or drafting a divorce petition.

In most cases, it will be appropriate to write a follow-up letter to the client summarising what has been discussed and agreed. Telling the client that you intend to do this is obviously reassuring.

If you have not already done so, now is a good time to check that you have an accurate note of the client's address and telephone number. Check also to which address the client wishes letters to be sent.

(3) Follow-up tasks by client

You should also remind the client of any action which he/she agreed to take. This might include supplying information or documents which were not available during the interview or thinking about the advice and contacting you once a decision has been reached.

(4) Time frame for the matter

The client should be given some indication of how long the matter will take to complete. Sometimes an estimate is quite easy to give:

> 'As the agreed terms are quite straightforward, I shall be able to send you and Simon a draft of the partnership agreement by the end of the week. Then, if you're both happy with it, it should be possible to sign the final document sometime during next week.'

In other cases, particularly where court proceedings are a possibility, it may be impossible to do more than give a very broad estimate because future developments will to a large extent be unpredictable and outside your control. Even in these situations, you should try to give some indication of time frame, even if it is only to indicate that the matter could potentially take years rather than months!

(5) Next contact

Make it clear which of you is to make the next contact. Does your client expect to hear from you or vice versa?

At the same time, tell your client whether you think that another face-to-face meeting will be necessary and (if so) why.

For example:

> 'So we've agreed that I shall do nothing until you let me know how much you want to offer to Mr Jones. I shall then write to his solicitors offering that sum in full and final settlement.
>
> Obviously, if they confirm in writing that he accepts, that will broadly be an end of the matter.

On the other hand, if he rejects the offer and continues with the court action, you and I will need to meet again to give more detailed consideration to the strength of the evidence in support of your defence.'

(6) Costs estimate of matter/method of charging

As stated in **10.5.4**, it will usually be possible to explain early in the interview how the interview itself is to be paid for, but seldom possible at that stage to discuss the likely cost of the matter itself. This will therefore usually be tackled as part of the closing stage of the interview, and care should be taken not to overlook it. The matters to be covered in the information to be given to the client are laid down in the 'Written Professional Standards (1999)'.

Broadly speaking, you must inform the client of:

(1) the likely overall costs;
(2) the basis of the firm's charges;
(3) whether the likely outcome will justify the expense.

For a more detailed study, see the LPC Resource Book *Pervasive and Core Topics* (Jordans) Part II, Professional Conduct.

Costs should be discussed in a business-like way.

You are providing a service to the client and should not therefore appear to be embarrassed at having to discuss money.

In many cases, particularly litigation, it will be necessary to make it clear to the client that only a rough estimate of the total cost can be given because of the uncertainty concerning the amount of work which may prove necessary and the time it will take. For example, 'If this matter can't be settled out of court and has to go to a full trial, the costs are likely to be well in excess of £10,000. At this stage, it's impossible to give you a precise estimate but I will report to you regularly about costs as the matter progresses'.

Skills summary
(1) Summarising (perhaps in writing)
(2) Explaining.

10.5.9 Parting

When the interview is over, you should accompany the client back to the reception area.

The parting should be friendly, courteous and (if possible) reassuring.

10.6 FURTHER READING

Students wishing to undertake further reading on the matters covered in this chapter will find any of the following books helpful.

Sherr *Client Care for Lawyers* 2nd edn (Sweet & Maxwell, 1999)
Twist *Effective Interviewing* (Blackstone Press, 1992)
Binder & Price *Legal Interviewing and Counselling* (West Publishing Co, USA, 1977)

Chapter 11

NEGOTIATION

11.1 INTRODUCTION

Solicitors spend much of their time negotiating in one way or another, whether in formal meetings to settle the terms of a company take-over or partnership agreement, or through a series of telephone calls to try to agree a mutually acceptable time and date for the completion of simultaneous conveyancing transactions.

The above two examples of negotiation are both transaction-based, ie, the parties are seeking to make an agreement or 'deal'. The other common type of negotiation is dispute resolution, where a dispute has already arisen between the parties giving rise to possible legal action (eg for breach of contract, negligence, undue influence on the making of a will, unfair dismissal, ancillary financial relief on divorce, breach of intellectual property rights). In such cases, resolving the dispute by negotiation rather than by litigation can save time and legal costs. It can also reduce animosity. This can be particularly important where the parties continue to have a relationship after the dispute has been resolved, such as a business relationship or a family one.

Whether it is transaction-based or dispute resolution, the general principles of negotiation remain the same but the specific application of those principles may vary according to the context. Negotiation is an art rather than a science.

Chapter 11 contents
Introduction
Aims of negotiation
The ethical aspects of negotiating
Negotiating styles
Preparation for a negotiation
Other considerations before a meeting
Overview of a negotiation
The opening
The middle phase: discussion and bargaining
The end: closing a negotiation
'Dirty tricks'
The forum for the negotiation
Alternative dispute resolution
Further reading

11.2 AIMS OF NEGOTIATION

Negotiation has been defined as 'a process of interaction by which two or more parties who consider they need to be jointly involved in an outcome, but who initially have different objectives, seek by the use of argument and persuasion to resolve their differences in order to achieve a mutually acceptable solution' (Alan Fowler, *Negotiation: Skills and Strategies* (IPM, 1990)).

This definition implies something different from the common perception of negotiating as a battle of wills, where necessarily one side wins at the expense of the other. Skilled negotiators are aware of the merits of achieving solutions that are seen by both sides as fair. They also realise that, by sharing as much information as possible with the other side, opportunities can arise to 'expand the cake' available to the parties. Such an approach does not mean that you accept a settlement which is against your client's best interests, but it does mean that you adopt a flexible approach; you should be open to ideas put forward by the other side and be prepared to adapt your position if new information comes to light in the negotiation.

Aspects of negotiating which this chapter seeks to encourage are:

- thorough preparation and the adoption of a logical approach when preparing for talks;
- the use of objective standards of reference when these are available (eg, audited accounts, experts' reports);

- the avoidance of an aggressive style. Experience suggests that a reasonable, polite approach is more likely to achieve results;
- searching for different (perhaps unconventional) solutions to problems;
- the promotion of trust between the parties;
- the production of settlements that will endure because they are perceived as fair by both (all) sides;
- the observance of high ethical standards.

11.3 THE ETHICAL ASPECTS OF NEGOTIATING

A solicitor must always act ethically in accordance with the solicitors' rules of professional conduct. A solicitor must never lie, for example by giving false information. However, there is no duty to volunteer information which is adverse to a client's position. If asked a direct question on such a point, the solicitor cannot lie, but he can refuse to answer, or offer no comment, or say 'I have no instructions on that point'. The other negotiator might then, of course, read between the lines of the reply and guess what the true position may be.

11.4 NEGOTIATING STYLES

11.4.1 Categories

Some writers group negotiators into two general styles with names like: hard/soft or aggressive/co-operative.

However, such categorisation can be a misleading division of a myriad of different styles. Figure 1 demonstrates this by charting two characteristics of the negotiator which are not necessarily mutually exclusive but which can be integrated with each other in widely varying degrees.

```
        HIGH
   A     |
   S     |
   S     |
   E     |
   R     |
   T     |
   I     |
   V     |
   E     |
         |_____ HIGH
   LOW         CO-OPERATIVE
```

Figure 1

How assertive are you? Mark your point on the vertical axis. How co-operative are you? Mark your point on the horizontal axis. Mark on the graph where your two points meet.

This analysis recognises that everybody's style is different: there are innumerable points on the graph. However, although it gives a general indication of a person's predominant style, the analysis still has inherent drawbacks. First, self-analysis is not always accurate. Secondly, it fails to recognise that you can and should vary your style according to the situation. Effective negotiators are highly flexible and will vary their style according to the merits of the case they are pursuing and the style adopted by the other negotiator.

```
              HIGH
               |
               | COMPETING              COLLABORATING
       A       |
       S       |
       S       |
       E       |
       R       |              COMPROMISING
       T       |
       I       |
       V       |
       E       |
               | AVOIDING               ACCOMMODATING
               |_____ HIGH
       LOW         CO-OPERATIVE
```

Figure 2

Figure 2 shows the same chart divided into five broad styles, any one of which can be used according to the circumstances.

It can be helpful to:

- know the potential strengths and weaknesses of your own predominant style;
- assess to what extent you can learn to vary your own style; and
- be able to identify, and react appropriately, to the style of the other negotiator.

11.4.2 Avoiding

The avoiding style is low both on assertiveness and co-operativeness. It is sometimes used by those who are facing actual or potential legal action, or a proposed term in a transaction, against which they have little or no argument. They hope that if they ignore the problem, either it will go away or circumstances will change in their favour.

It is also an approach that might be adopted by the solicitor on one side if he knows the other side has a deadline to meet. He will be trying to put off the real negotiations until the other side is under severe time pressure, knowing that this will then put him into a strong position.

The appropriate response to an opponent who adopts an avoiding style is to press ahead as quickly as possible, perhaps by imposing time-limits on him or by pursuing alternative courses of action which force him into serious talks, for example by serving a writ.

11.4.3 Accommodating

A person adopting an accommodating style is too ready to accept the other side's proposals and accept an agreement which might not be in his client's best interests. It is normally a style which stems from the negotiator's personality rather than one which is being used deliberately.

It may be consciously adopted, however, if the other side has grossly misjudged the parties' positions and you are only too happy to accommodate them. Even in these circumstances though, it might be wiser not to take advantage of the other side's error, especially when the parties will have an ongoing relationship.

11.4.4 Compromising

It is vital that negotiators should have the capacity to compromise; otherwise, deals would never be made and disputes would never be settled. A party may be prepared to compromise in order to avoid:

- the uncertainties of trial (on liability or quantum, or witnesses not coming 'up to proof');
- the delay involved in going to trial;
- the emotional stress that continued litigation could involve;
- the legal costs of going any further – even if you win in court, you are unlikely to recover all the legal costs from the unsuccessful defendant;
- the further loss of management time for a commercial client;
- the transaction falling through; or
- souring an ongoing relationship between two commercial parties or between members of a family.

The question is how and when to compromise. A compromising style might be characterised by a readiness always to 'split the difference' between the two sides' positions, regardless of the objective merits. There may sometimes be good reasons for closing the deal in this way, but they do not include the easy disposal of the matter or the speedier payment of your fees.

11.4.5 Competing

Competitors are unco-operative and highly assertive. They may or may not also be aggressive.

If you have a strong case and the other side is accommodating, a competing style can be highly effective.

On the other hand, if it is misused, the style can create mistrust, distorted communication, tension and the souring of long-term relationships. It can provoke retaliation (the other side becomes aggressive) or obstinacy (the other side digs in his heels). In either case, settlement can be severely delayed or a proposed deal can fall apart. Clients will not be grateful.

If you are faced with competitive negotiators, try to avoid counter-productive reactions. Ignore the personality and concentrate on the objective merits of the arguments. It may be helpful to ask yourself: 'Why are they behaving like this?' There could be a number of possible reasons, each of which should generate a different response from you.

(1) The behaviour might be part of their personality, their normal style. Have you or any of your colleagues negotiated with them before? Consult as widely as possible.

(2) It may be that they do in fact have a very strong case.

(3) They may have a very weak case and are therefore bluffing or over-compensating. Stay calm. Take care not to react too hastily. Bide your time until you are more certain of the objective merits of the case.

(4) They may be under-prepared. As a result, they may be worried that they are running the risk of making an error of judgement and conceding too much. They therefore over-compensate and become less co-operative and more assertive (or avoiding) in order to reduce that risk. If you suspect this to be the reason, the best tactic might be to adjourn the negotiation until they are better prepared.

(5) They may have become competitive in response to what they perceive to be your competitiveness. There is anecdotal evidence that, after a heated and unproductive negotiation, one negotiator said to a neutral observer: 'I started off in a spirit of co-operation and compromise; I was prepared to adopt a collaborative search for a mutually acceptable solution; but he was so competitive that we both ended up just going hammer and tongs at each other'. The other negotiator said exactly the same.

Ultimately, it should be remembered that in a negotiation there are no rules or procedures which have to be followed (unless you have agreed to them) and there is no obligation to reach a settlement. The other side cannot force you into anything without your consent.

11.4.6 Collaborating

Some people call collaboration 'problem-solving' or 'principled negotiation'. In theory, it is often the ideal negotiating style because it gives you the best of both worlds. Assertiveness and co-operativeness are not mutually exclusive. You can be high in both.

Assertiveness is not the same as aggression. You should aim to be sufficiently assertive to press your own client's case and to avoid being trampled on by an aggressive opponent; at the same time, you should be sufficiently co-operative to search for any possibility of a mutually beneficial solution. This is particularly important where there will be (or the parties would like there to be) a continuing business or personal relationship after the present dispute has been resolved.

Beware, however, of certain risks.

(1) Beware of wolves in sheep's clothing, ie, the pleasant negotiator who smiles a lot, flatters you, appears to be perfectly reasonable (and may pepper his statements with phrases like 'fair and reasonable' and 'sympathetic to your client's case'), but who on objective analysis is being competitive and offering very little. The moral is: do not jump to conclusions; try not to allow personality to influence you; concentrate on the objective merits of the case.

(2) If you are trying to adjust your own predominant style, for example become more assertive or become more co-operative, there is a danger that, as one characteristic increases, so the other decreases. Although it is possible to be high on both, it can be difficult to achieve.

11.4.7 Conclusion

Everyone has elements of all five styles within them. You should try to be flexible, to exploit your strengths, to minimise your weaknesses, and not to be distracted by personalities. Do not allow your own ego to intrude. Try to think about the case objectively from your client's point of view.

The rest of this chapter generally assumes a collaborative style. However, thorough preparation, self-confidence and perceptiveness are more important than personal style.

11.5 PREPARATION FOR A NEGOTIATION

11.5.1 Importance of preparation

The successful negotiator possesses many skills; these include the ability to communicate, listen, persuade, analyse and create. These talents must, however, be supported by a bedrock of knowledge.

A thorough knowledge of the facts, the law and the procedure relevant to a particular case is vital. Without that knowledge, you lose any chance of controlling the negotiating process.

It is also essential to establish clearly your client's objectives in entering into the negotiation. What is the minimum he is prepared to accept? Has he reached this position with the benefit of all available information? If he is proceeding under certain misconceptions, it is part of your role to correct them.

Armed with the requisite knowledge (law, facts and procedure) and your client's instructions, a plan based on the following sections (**11.5.2–11.5.7**) should be prepared.

11.5.2 Interests not positions

Invariably, the client will inform you of his negotiating position; he wants compensation, a fixed-term contract, the removal of a tenant. You must look behind his stated position and try to identify his underlying interests. Why does the client want what he is demanding? Ask – otherwise you may end up negotiating on the basis of false assumptions.

What are the other side's interests in entering into the negotiation? Some consideration of what these might be can help you to avoid being taken by surprise in the talks.

In addition, once the underlying interests or unspoken assumptions are identified, it may be that the underlying interests can be satisfied in some other way and at less cost than you initially expected.

> *Example*
> In negotiating a lease of the major unit in a new shopping mall, the landlord might demand from his major 'anchor' tenant absolute bars on assignment, subletting or change of use. The tenant might demand absolute freedom on all three. This presents an apparent impasse. However, the landlord's underlying

interest might be to use the anchor tenant to attract 'satellite' tenants to the other, smaller units, while the tenant's interest might be the long-term freedom to move elsewhere. A compromise which might satisfy both parties' underlying interests would be to have a short-term restriction rather than one which lasts for the whole duration of the lease.

Looking for underlying interests is particularly important in transaction-based negotiations or multi-issue claims. It is less likely to be productive in debt collection, personal injury or other single issue, 'money only' claims. However, it should always be investigated. For example, in debt collection it may be that the creditor has an underlying interest in the survival of the debtor's business.

11.5.3 Strengths and weaknesses

The logical next step after a consideration of the parties' underlying interests is to assess the factors which support and those which undermine your client's case (ie, once you know what he wants, what are the chances of him getting what he wants?).

Identify your client's strengths and the other side's weaknesses. Perhaps your client has no pressing need to make a deal but the other side has financial difficulties which make it vital for him to reach an agreement; perhaps your client's case is supported by strong legal precedent.

What are the other side's strengths? Is there anything you can do to counter them? For example, can you obtain other evidence or reinterpret existing evidence?

What are the weaknesses in the other side's position? For example, will he risk court action if his main concern is to avoid bad publicity?

Expect the other side to have spotted the weaknesses in your client's case and to ask questions that could expose those weaknesses. Anticipate these questions and prepare carefully worded replies which (without lying or misrepresenting the position), as far as possible, protect your client.

You must, of course, behave ethically. Any misrepresentation would constitute professional misconduct, as well as rendering voidable any resulting agreement.

What questions could you ask to exploit your client's strengths and which probe for weaknesses in the other side's position? The phrasing of such questions should be carefully considered to make it difficult for the other side to avoid giving a straight (and hopefully revealing) answer.

To negotiate effectively you must be assertive in advancing your client's case and tenacious in seeking replies to your questions. However, this should be done within the constraints of a professional and detached approach. If the general tone of your questioning (or answers) is aggressive, sarcastic or discourteous, it is likely to sour relationships and prevent you from having productive discussions.

11.5.4 BATNA

One of the best-known books on negotiation is Fisher and Ury's *Getting to Yes*. Their acronym, BATNA, stands for Best Alternative To a Negotiated Agreement. In other words, *if the negotiations were to break down and you fail to settle*, what would you be left with? What would be the true cost or value of that alternative?

In transaction cases, your BATNA could be to do a deal with a third party rather than with the other side, or not to do a deal at all. In dispute resolution cases, the BATNA would often be litigation. Exploring the available alternatives in advance can concentrate the mind wonderfully – both your own mind and your client's. Make sure that the perceived BATNA is a realistic alternative and not just a vague possibility.

Fisher and Ury recommend that you identify, evaluate and develop your own BATNA and also try to guess the other side's. Developing your own BATNA might involve, for example, pressing ahead with litigation procedures simultaneously with trying to negotiate an out-of-court settlement.

The aim of the BATNA approach to planning a negotiation is to provide you with a yardstick against which you can assess the value of any offer made in the negotiation. Identifying your BATNA helps you to decide your 'resistance point' in the negotiation (see **11.5.5**). It can therefore protect you from being too generous, ie agreeing to give the other side more than the value of your BATNA. It can also protect you from being too obstinate, ie rejecting a final offer which is in fact better than your BATNA.

If your client appears to have an attractive alternative available, this strengthens his negotiating position; it might, therefore, be a good tactic to make the other side aware of this alternative.

In some instances, the client may have more than one alternative course of action available. If so, you should discuss with your client the feasibility of each alternative and consider whether it is worthwhile trying to develop each alternative or to concentrate on just one.

11.5.5 Issues, priorities and variables

(1) Isolation of separate issues

Many negotiations involve the resolution of several issues. It is a good idea in such cases to isolate each issue. One reason for doing this is that it helps to ensure that all relevant matters are covered in the negotiation.

> *Example*
> Your client is a retailer who has a contract with a manufacturer for the supply of an exclusive range of golfing accessories. The client has suffered losses owing to the manufacturer failing to meet agreed supply dates. He wants compensation but is aware that the stocking of the contract goods generates a great deal of his custom.
>
> The issues are:
>
> - the claim for compensation;
>
> - the continuation of a profitable relationship.

(2) Relative importance of each issue

Secondly, a discussion with your client on the relative importance to him of each issue allows you to have a clear view of his priorities. In the above example, your client would almost certainly decide that the claim for compensation should not be pressed too hard if it would put at risk the continuation of the relationship.

(3) Opening bids and resistance points

On each issue, make an assessment of the most favourable result that you would hope to achieve and the least favourable result that you are likely to accept.

MOST FAVOURABLE RESULT ('OPENING BID')

To begin by making demands which are wildly optimistic and which bear no relation to the parties' positions will result in you losing credibility. You are bound to look foolish when you are unable to give sound reasons to justify your position.

The bid you make should be the highest justifiable bid, after taking into account the law and facts which support your client's case; ie, try to predict the settlement you would obtain if all the factors which support your case were accepted, without any counter-arguments being put forward by the other side.

> *Example*
> Through no fault of his own, your client has been dismissed by his employer, with 2 years of a fixed-term contract left to run. His salary (after tax and national insurance deductions) was £35,000 per annum. The most favourable result would be to obtain the total of lost net salary (£70,000) for the remaining 2-year period. It is a bid which can be justified on a contractual basis.
>
> You would expect your opponent to put forward arguments which support the reduction of this figure (eg the former employee has a duty to mitigate his loss by looking for other work), but if he fails to do so you could achieve a very good settlement for your client (although, bear in mind that other factors may lead you to decide not to take advantage of the other side's mistakes).

This is one of the possible benefits of aiming high at the start. Another is that if valid counter-arguments are raised, it allows you to 'come down' and offer concessions. This can be an important way of showing the other side that you have listened to and understood their case and that you are prepared to compromise. Any compromise requires 'give and take'. It allows people to save face; honour is satisfied. If, however, you refuse to move from your opening figure, the other side may perceive you as obstinate and unreasonable, and therefore might refuse to settle even when your opening figure is in fact realistic.

Generally, you should only open at your final figure if:

- it is the tradition or culture in that particular field of law; or
- you have a case or bargaining position that is not only strong, but obviously strong.

In either case, you should explain clearly to the other side that it really is a case of take it or leave it.

LEAST FAVOURABLE RESULT THAT, ON CURRENT INFORMATION, YOU WOULD ACCEPT ('RESISTANCE POINT')

The above process can also allow you to decide on the poorest deal your client should accept, ie, what settlement you would expect to negotiate if the other side puts forward all the relevant counter-arguments to your client's case.

The resistance point is not a 'bottom line'; it should not be rigidly adhered to if further information which affects your client's position comes to light in the negotiation. You must be flexible enough to take on board the significance of any new information and adapt your expectations accordingly.

Deciding on the resistance point is complicated by two other factors. First, in cases where your client has an acceptable alternative course of action, the resistance point is the point below which the client is likely to receive less from the negotiation than could be obtained by pursuing the BATNA. For example, you might decide that (even after taking into account the extra costs) your client would receive more than is currently being offered by allowing the court to decide on the level of compensation.

Secondly, your client may have given you instructions not to settle below a certain figure. If you think he is being unrealistic you should try to persuade him to adopt a more sensible position, but if he cannot be moved you must comply with his instructions.

With multi-issue negotiations, the position becomes even more complicated. You might be prepared to go below your resistance point on one issue if it means you would obtain a favourable result on another. It is important to keep the whole package in mind.

Your client's priorities are the key to the decisions you make in this area. Items which are of no great significance to your client could be conceded altogether in exchange for concessions which are of more importance to him.

(4) *Variables and unorthodox approaches*

Another consideration in assessing the opening bid and resistance point will be the existence of 'variables'. Variables are those factors which allow for some give and take in the negotiation and which could therefore help to achieve a settlement. For example, your client might be prepared to pay a higher amount of compensation if she is allowed to pay by instalments rather than in one lump sum.

Other examples of variables which can be brought into play (depending on the subject matter of the negotiation) are inclusion/exclusion of costs, payment in a different currency, promises of future orders, quantity of goods (eg buy more, but at a lower price per unit), quality of goods (eg buy a lower grade at a lower price).

Sometimes, there may be other (perhaps unconventional) ways to resolve problems which have benefits for both sides. In Fisher and Ury's terms, you should try to 'invent options for mutual gain'.

> *Example*
> You are acting for a business which runs a parcel delivery service. One of its business customers is threatening to take action against your client because of its failure to deliver a consignment of goods. The goods have disappeared and the customer is asking for compensation. An orthodox settlement would involve a cash payment to the customer. A different approach would be to offer to make free deliveries for that customer over an agreed period. Such an offer could represent a good deal for the customer but could still be a cheaper solution for your client compared to a cash payment (the deliveries could probably be accommodated within its regular delivery service and so would not add greatly to overall costs). This approach also gives your client a chance to rebuild the customer's confidence in its service, making it less likely that the customer will go elsewhere in the future.

11.5.6 Prediction of the result (settlement zones)

Can you identify a possible settlement zone? The planning in **11.5.1–11.5.5** all leads to this. You can only decide on your final strategy if you have already worked through those stages. Your final strategy must use them and be consistent with them.

Identifying a possible settlement zone involves:

(1) deciding on:

- your client's opening bid; and
- his current resistance point (ie, the process described in **11.5.5**. Avoid the creation of false expectations on your client's part by ensuring that he appreciates the difference between a resistance point and a bottom line);

(2) making an educated guess at the other side's opening bid and resistance point;
(3) in the negotiation, constantly re-assessing (1) and (2) in the light of new information.

The settlement zone, if it exists at all, lies between the resistance points of the two sides. All negotiators go through the above process, more or less consciously, but it is helpful to do so methodically.

Example

In the above example of the dismissed employee, it was established that his opening bid should be in the region of £70,000. Assume that his solicitor has advised him that the least favourable result he would expect is a payment of £20,000 (taking into account the duty to mitigate the loss and the current job market for the client's skills). The employer, on the other hand, has been advised that a payment of £17,500 is probably the best result it could hope to achieve but it is prepared to pay up to £35,000, if necessary, to avoid any bad publicity that the case might generate and so that management time is not wasted on preparation for a court action.

As illustrated by *Figure 3*, the settlement zone is between £20,000 and £35,000.

```
EMPLOYER    OPENING                    RESISTANCE
            BID                        POINT
            £17,500                    £35,000
                    |--------------------------|
                    |     SETTLEMENT           |
                    |     ZONE                 |
                    |--------------------------|
                    £20,000                    £70,000
EMPLOYEE            RESISTANCE                 OPENING
                    POINT                      BID
```

Figure 3

(4) Having identified the settlement zone, try to predict the result you would expect to achieve on all of the relevant issues, bearing in mind the respective positions of the parties.

11.5.7 Opening statement

When you have reached a decision on your negotiating strategy, you are then in a position to decide on the content of your opening statement.

There are several points to consider (see **11.8.3**), but a basic consideration at the preparatory stage is to decide upon the information you would want to disclose to the other side at this early point in the talks.

In most cases, the more information you communicate to the other side the better the chance of reaching an agreement. In particular, there are usually interests which are common to both sides; these should be stressed at the start.

The sharing of information develops trust between the parties and helps to create the climate for successful talks.

There will, however, be some information that you correctly decide not to reveal, either because it is damaging to your client's position (in which case you would hope to avoid disclosing it at any stage) or because you would prefer to introduce it later for tactical reasons (eg you intend to put it forward as a concession to the other side at the bargaining stage).

11.6 OTHER CONSIDERATIONS BEFORE A MEETING

11.6.1 Are you ready to negotiate?

Do not be forced into premature negotiations. It is usually advisable to defer talks until you are in possession of all the information you can reasonably expect to collect.

11.6.2 Venue

In some fields of law, there is a tradition that meetings will take place at the offices of the seller or claimant. What if you have a choice? What are the factors to bear in mind?

Having the meeting at your own firm's premises gives you the feeling of control. You have full access to your papers and to the office's secretarial, catering and other facilities. Also, you do not have to suffer the time, cost and general inconvenience of having to travel.

Attending a meeting at the other side's offices might therefore be a disadvantage. However, the travelling time can sometimes enable you to arrive fresher and more fully prepared. Also, enabling the other side to feel at ease in their own offices might induce them to be more collaborative.

A third possibility is to agree a neutral venue.

11.6.3 Agree the time and length of the meeting

As a matter of courtesy to the other side, you should inform them of the time you can devote to the meeting on the agreed date.

11.6.4 Attendance at the meeting

How many people from each side will be attending? Find out their names and roles in advance. If a number of people will be attending, who will chair the meeting – the host, the person who suggested the meeting, or some other person?

Will clients also be present? Often, they are present at transaction-based negotiations but not at litigation-based meetings. Sometimes clients sit in separate side-rooms or make themselves available for telephone calls or faxes in order to give instructions to their solicitors during the meeting.

It may be a good idea to have clients present at the meeting so that an agreement can be hammered out there and then, particularly if you think:

- the major problem has been a lack of communication between the respective clients; or
- your own client is being unrealistic; or
- the other solicitor is the problem (eg not settling a case which his or her client wants to settle); and
- you can trust your own client (preparation of roles is vital); and
- you trust the other solicitor not to seek to undermine your authority in front of your own client.

Conversely, you might not wish to have clients present where there are personality clashes between the different clients or where you have an intimidating client who might hamper your style.

11.6.5 Seating arrangements

Who will sit where? What ambience do you want to try to create? To sit face to face across a table from each other is more likely to appear adversarial, whereas seating placed at a 90 degree angle is likely to appear more collaborative.

11.6.6 Clarify the purpose of the meeting

Is the meeting to be exploratory only, or is there a possibility of settling? If the latter, check that those attending will have authority to settle on behalf of their respective clients.

11.6.7 The agenda

In a multi-issue case, try to agree the agenda with the other side in advance.

If possible, try to arrange the order of issues on the agenda in a way which will enable you to test their negotiating pattern and their willingness to trade concessions before reaching an item which is of critical importance to your own client.

11.6.8 Decide your strategy

Examples of matters you might like to consider are:

- your opening position;
- the amount and the sequence of the concessions you might be prepared to offer; and
- what disclosures to make and when.

However, you should be prepared to be flexible.

11.6.9 Which party should make the first bid?

In some fields of law, the issue of which person makes the first bid is determined partly by tradition. For example, in property transactions, the solicitor acting for the landlord or seller draws up the draft lease or contract. In litigation, if the claim is for a liquidated sum (eg a contractual debt), the opening bid belongs to the claimant. If the claim is for unliquidated damages, in certain cases (eg personal injury claims) there is an argument that the claimant should simply wait until the defendant makes an acceptable Part 36 offer or payment.

Where the position is not clear-cut, the advantages of going first are that it allows you to exert an immediate and powerful influence and it shows confidence. The disadvantage is that you risk misjudging the bid.

Even if you do not wish to make the first bid, you might still like to make the first opening statement, so that you can try to establish the climate of the negotiation.

11.6.10 Final preparation for the meeting

Reread the file, and refresh your mind on key documents, facts, dates and names.

Make sure that you know your client's position on the issues and on all the possible variables.

11.7 OVERVIEW OF A NEGOTIATION

Every negotiation should have a beginning, a middle and an end. It should be an agreed, structured process (like the order of advocacy in court hearings); otherwise, there is the risk that it will degenerate into chaos, with continual sniping and cross-fire. As a general principle, the wheels of a negotiation are oiled by good structure and management. As with interviewing and advising, structure and management interrelate with personal communication skills: each promotes the other.

Structure	*A possible strategy*
Opening	Aiming high
Discussion and bargaining	Probing Searching for variables Trading concessions Keeping whole package in mind
Closing	

11.8 THE OPENING

11.8.1 Creating the climate

The opening phase of a negotiation is important for two reasons. First, it creates the climate for the negotiation. Patterns, styles and pecking order establish themselves early and are difficult then to change.

Secondly, energy and concentration are high at the outset of the negotiations but later deteriorate.

11.8.2 Ground rules

The host of the meeting should, after effecting any necessary introductions, confirm the ground rules for the meeting, for example:

- the purpose of the meeting;
- whether or not it is 'without prejudice' and/or 'subject to contract';
- the likely length of the meeting;
- the agenda; and
- who will make the first opening statement.

11.8.3 Your opening statement

Proper, well-prepared opening statements are a great help to most negotiation meetings. They:

- help to reinforce the climate established at the outset of the meeting;
- provide structure and order (an analogy can be drawn with court trials – the advocates' opening addresses set the scene; cross-examination etc comes later);
- help everyone to 'settle down';
- remind everyone of the background, the areas of agreement, and the areas of dispute;
- help to avoid unintentional false assumptions from hindering the communication process.

Unless you have sound tactical reasons for not following them, there are some general rules relating to opening statements.

Do:
- consider saying how long your statement will take, if it is likely to be more than two or three minutes;
- if your opening statement is going to contain a bid, explain your reasoning *before* disclosing the actual bid. This increases the chances of the other side listening properly to your reasons. Otherwise, they will be thinking about the figure and their response rather than your reasons;
- present your case concisely and confidently;
- use collaborative tone, posture and gestures (unless you have decided to adopt a competitive style);
- observe carefully the other side's verbal and non-verbal reactions;
- remember the one-third rule (see **9.1**).

Don't:
- express your assumptions of the other side's interests and priorities, as this could annoy or antagonise them. Allow them to make their own case in their opening statement;
- allow them to interrupt or side-track you;
- speak for too long.

11.8.4 The other side's opening statement

It is important that you:
- listen carefully – use all the passive listening techniques (see **9.2.1**);
- concentrate on identifying their underlying interests;
- evaluate their style;
- remain non-committal on their proposals and arguments – indicate understanding, if you can, without indicating agreement;
- take brief notes (this can be a useful way of concealing your immediate reactions).

At the end of their opening statement:
- seek clarification if necessary. Do not allow pride to deter you – you must be sure you understand exactly what they are saying. Negotiations can easily break down because of simple miscommunication;
- summarise;
- stress areas of agreement;
- make sure that they have told you the whole of their 'shopping list', to reduce the risk of being ambushed later by a last-minute demand.

Do not concentrate too much on mentally drafting or rehearsing your own rebuttal, as this will hinder your listening to and understanding their case, and do not interrupt (unless you have deliberately chosen to be competitive).

11.9 THE MIDDLE PHASE: DISCUSSION AND BARGAINING

> Statements generate resistance
> Questions generate answers
> Silence generates discomfort, answers, new suggestions.
> (adapted from a passage in *Getting to Yes* by Fisher and Ury)

> 'I don't go in to do all the talking. Quite the opposite.
> I go in to do the listening because that's the best bit.'
> (Insurance company chief claims inspector, quoted in *Hard Bargaining* by Hazel Genn)

11.9.1 Discussion

During the discussion:

(1) demonstrate that you have heard and understood what the other side has said even if you do not agree with them;

(2) in the middle phase of a negotiation, you should probe the other side's case with a mixture of appropriate open and closed questions.

You could question any of the following:

- any assumptions you think they might be making;
- their underlying interests or needs ('Why does your client want ... ?');
- whether or not there may be other ways of meeting those interests;
- the criteria or evidence to justify their bid ('What criteria did you use to arrive at ... ?' 'What evidence have you got to support ... ?' 'Where did you get that evidence from?');
- their interpretation of the law or of the facts; or
- analogous or comparable circumstances or cases they have had.

Do not ask two questions at once.

Give them time to answer – do not be tempted to fill a silence too quickly.

Listen and observe carefully when they answer. Was there any hesitation, uncertainty or discomfort?

If necessary, re-phrase crucial questions so that all the angles are covered.

Do not allow them to use diversionary tactics such as answering a question with a question, or changing the subject. Be courteous but firm;

(3) spell out the weaknesses of their position calmly and firmly;

(4) be prepared to answer their questions with a judicious mixture of firm replies, silences and counter-questions. Try to maintain a confident tone of voice and posture;

(5) review the progress of the discussions at appropriate intervals. If there is an impasse, or one aspect is taking too long, consider the following:

- defer further discussion of the particular topic until later in the negotiation;
- summarise. This can give you the opportunity to stress the areas on which you have already reached agreement and so reinforce the climate for agreement; it can also give you time to think and, if appropriate, to try to redirect the negotiation;

(6) explore the possibility of settling issues on the basis of objective criteria. For example, you might agree to accept the opinion of an independent expert as a way to resolve the problem. An advantage of this approach is that neither party can feel cheated by the other; another is that you are more likely to achieve a fair result, which can have particular benefits where the parties will have an ongoing relationship.

11.9.2 Bargaining

Generally, you will only have agreed to a meeting (other than a purely exploratory meeting) if both parties are prepared to compromise, ie, to bargain.

Although you might bargain item by item or clause by clause in multi-issue cases, try to keep the whole package in mind. It might be sensible not to finalise an agreement on any particular issue until the shape of the whole agreement is clear (including, for example, costs).

Keep searching for variables, for example: time for payment; payment in a different currency; a promise of future orders or the grant of options; performance-related payments; performance in stages.

Bargaining involves the trading of concessions. Compromise is achieved by both parties moving from their original positions. On the assumption that the other side has aimed high, you should be reluctant to accept their first offer.

A competitive negotiator might refuse to concede anything to you for some time, and then concede only small amounts, slowly and at irregular intervals, and of diminishing amounts. Such a strategy is clearly designed to lower your expectations. However, if in fact there is a significant margin between that negotiator's opening bid and resistance point, the strategy carries the risk of a relatively sudden but very late climb-down (eg a 'door-of-the-court' settlement). If you suspect that this strategy is being used against you, consider abbreviating the negotiation and press ahead with your BATNA (Best Alternative To a Negotiated Agreement) – for example, by pressing ahead with the litigation if you are a claimant or making a Part 36 payment if you are a defendant.

When you are offered a concession, it is a question of judgement whether you express appreciation for it, or emphasise the lack of cost to them, or both.

When making a concession, emphasise the cost to you of it and try to give a reason for it. For example, you can often relate it to something the other side has said in the negotiation. Your concession can thus demonstrate that you have taken their point and responded accordingly, rather than appear to be arbitrary.

In order to avoid 'giving away' a concession with nothing in return, or in order to try to move the negotiation forward, always consider offering conditional or hypothetical concessions: 'We could move on X but only if you could move on Y'; 'I have no authority from my client on this point, but what if X?'. Although these statements might be interpreted to mean that, if pushed, you would be prepared to concede unreservedly, it is a risk that parties have to take in the dynamics of a negotiation.

Make sure you take appropriate notes and, in particular, keep a record of all concessions or agreements.

11.9.3 Adjournments

Adjournments can be very useful.

The length of an adjournment will depend on its purpose. It could be for as little as ten minutes, for example, in order to have a brief strategy review (on your own, with a colleague, or with your client), or for as long as several weeks or months in order to await the availability of further evidence.

Other reasons for suggesting an adjournment include:

- alertness waning;
- to help resolve an impasse or deadlock;
- to allow a heated atmosphere to cool down; or
- to try to 'close the deal' during the relative informality of a refreshment break.

11.9.4 Resolving deadlocks

In cases of deadlock, the following actions should be considered:

- defer an item on the agenda;
- search for variables;

- adjourn; or
- refer to an alternative dispute resolution ('ADR') process (see **11.13**).

11.10 THE END: CLOSING A NEGOTIATION

11.10.1 When?

The timing of the close of a negotiation will depend on a cost-benefit analysis. How much more do you think you can achieve? Compare the expected achievements against the cost to the client in terms of time, money and stress. Will further negotiation be cost effective? This analysis needs to be conducted at regular intervals. Beware of a variation of Parkinson's Law: 'negotiating expands to fill the time allotted to it'.

11.10.2 How?

A number of tactics can be used to signal to the other side that you see the end in sight.

- 'Last rites' – summarise the position reached, emphasising the concessions you have made and the extent and reasonableness of your movement: 'We have reached our final position';
- Use a refreshment break to suggest informally that the end is near;
- Give a deadline or ultimatum;
- Make a concession and express it as a final gesture to settle;
- If the gap between the sides is small, either suggest, or try to induce the other side to suggest, that you 'split the difference';
- If there is one outstanding point, you might be able to agree that the point be adjudicated by an agreed independent third party.

11.10.3 The agreement

Do not allow the euphoria of reaching agreement to distract you from other important and immediate tasks, such as:

- confirming what has been agreed;
- preparing an immediate agreed written summary;
- ensuring that details are clarified in order to avoid later disputes; and
- preparing a list of actions to be taken (if appropriate) by both sides.

11.11 'DIRTY TRICKS'

The phrase 'dirty tricks' is used loosely, and is not necessarily confined to misconduct. You need to be aware of such tricks, not so that you can use them, but in order to both be able to recognise them when they are used against you and, if possible, be able to counter them. They include the following.

11.11.1 Surprise attacks

Surprise attacks can take the form of sudden changes in tactics or demands, intimidation, withdrawal of offers or emotional outbursts. They are often designed to throw you off balance, undermine your confidence, and create anxiety and a desire to placate or settle quickly.

Try to remain unperturbed. Try not to retaliate. If you find it difficult to continue to focus on the merits of the case, consider questioning the other side's tactics openly or calling an adjournment.

11.11.2 'Good guy, bad guy'

The 'good guy, bad guy' tactic is sometimes used by a negotiating team of lawyers, or a solicitor who wishes to portray his client as hard and uncompromising.

The aim of the tactic is to capitalise on the relief felt at evading the 'bad guy'. Again, you should try to continue to focus on the merits of the case.

11.11.3 Feinting

Feinting is where the solicitor seems to attach great importance to one particular item. He then concedes it in order to 'soften you up' for another item in which he expresses little interest but which is, in fact, far more important to his client.

Do not take things at face value.

11.11.4 False deadlines

False deadlines can sometimes be tested by saying 'We might be able to offer more, but we will not know until after [the date of the deadline]'.

11.11.5 Limited authority/reneging on 'agreements'

Always make sure at the time of the agreement that it is explicit whether or not the solicitor has the authority to settle, whether the agreement is final, and record the position in writing. If you do not, you may think that a case has been settled only to receive a letter stating, for example: 'I reported on our provisional agreement. My client is fairly happy with it, but there is just one matter …'.

11.11.6 Last-minute demands

Make sure you obtain all the other side's demands at the outset. This will make it less likely that they will surprise you with a sudden new demand.

11.11.7 Environmental controls

If the seating arrangements or environment of the meeting room make you feel uncomfortable, you should immediately and politely ask for them to be changed.

11.11.8 Lying

Try to take accurate notes of key points without being distracted from the negotiation. If you can later prove that the other side lied during the negotiation, then the settlement could be rescinded for misrepresentation and, where a solicitor knowingly lied, the matter could be reported to The Law Society as professional misconduct.

11.12 THE FORUM FOR THE NEGOTIATION

The forum for negotiation could be correspondence, telephone, a meeting or any combination of the three.

At the outset, choose the most appropriate medium for your client's case, and then be prepared to change if it proves appropriate. For example, in many cases you might start by using correspondence, but that could later become unnecessarily rigid and time-consuming. It may be wise to suggest a meeting when you have developed a strong enough case to be able to take advantage of face-to-face contact.

Correspondence

Correspondence has the following features:

- it is capable of being orderly and reasoned, and is therefore especially appropriate at the outset of complex cases;
- it gives people time to think and therefore to avoid over-hasty decisions;
- there is a risk that certain points in a letter may be left unanswered in the reply;
- some solicitors find it easier to be assertive;
- it contains no non-verbal signals ('body language');
- it can lead to delay – either as a tactic, or because ambiguities or omissions are not rectified immediately;
- it is more difficult to trade concessions.

Telephone

Negotiation conducted by telephone has the following features:

- it is quick and useful for resolving one point;
- make sure you are properly prepared. It is better to be the person making the call. If you are the receiver, consider saying that you will call back at an agreed time so that you have the opportunity to prepare properly;
- there is no body language, but tones of voice are more noticeable. Silences are even more powerful on the telephone than in meetings. Use silence yourself, and do not be tempted to fill silences with a remark you may regret;
- some solicitors find it more difficult to be assertive on the telephone than in correspondence; some find it is the other way round;
- there is a risk that either of the parties could subsequently 're-interpret' what was said.

Meetings

Meetings have the following features:

- they are immediate;
- they give greater commitment to explore the case thoroughly and/or to settle;
- body language and silences are readily apparent and capable of use;
- they are more fluid and give greater possibilities of fine movements, nuances, and the trading of concessions;
- some solicitors regard the suggestion of a meeting as a sign of weakness; others regard it as a sign of strength.

Some solicitors have a fear of meetings because of the possibility of making a decision which is later regretted, or accidentally revealing a weakness, or generally feeling uncomfortable in a potentially adversarial face-to-face role. All of this is quite natural. If, however, a meeting would objectively be in the client's best interests, you should try to overcome any fears by thorough preparation and practice which will increase your self-confidence.

11.13 ALTERNATIVE DISPUTE RESOLUTION

11.13.1 What is it?

Alternative dispute resolution (ADR) is not a term of art: it is simply any process of dispute resolution other than litigation, arbitration or traditional negotiation between the parties or their solicitors.

The object of litigation, arbitration, negotiation or ADR is to provide a process which efficiently and effectively resolves a dispute. Which of the four, or which combination of them is best, will depend on the circumstances of each case.

The essential ingredients of ADR are:

(1) it is a voluntary, private process. The parties cannot be forced to use ADR; if they do use it, they can control the mechanics and rules of the process; and they can withdraw from it at any time unless and until they make a contractually binding out-of-court settlement or agreement;
(2) there is a third party neutral (often a mediator) who facilitates settlement, often by 'shuttlecock' diplomacy, but who has no power to order or impose a solution on the parties.

In essence, ADR is intended to be an efficient and structured form of negotiation involving a third party. It can thus be interposed between traditional negotiating and litigation (or arbitration): if traditional negotiating fails, try an ADR process; if that fails, then either stalemate or litigation (or arbitration) remains.

Although usually used in the litigation field, ADR can also be used in commercial transactions. First, a commercial contract could incorporate an ADR clause, ie, a non-binding (but influential) promise that if any dispute later arises between the parties, they will refer that dispute to an ADR process before resorting to litigation or arbitration.

Secondly, if parties are negotiating the terms of a transaction and reach an impasse on one particular term, they could agree to refer that one item to an ADR process.

11.13.2 The advantages

Like traditional negotiating, ADR can be quicker, cheaper and more private, and produce more flexible terms of settlement, than litigation or arbitration.

The third party neutral:

- can provide a view that is perceived by both parties as being more objective;
- by shuttlecock diplomacy may be able to identify potential solutions that neither party alone could see; and
- has a better chance of preserving relationships between the parties.

This last point can be very important in commercial or family disputes, but is less so where neither party has any intention of continuing any future relationship with the other.

11.13.3 The disadvantages

(1) One reason why ADR is relatively quick and cheap is that the evidence is not investigated or examined as thoroughly as in litigation or arbitration: instead, only what are thought to be the key issues and interests are explored. Parties cannot have it both ways, ie, a wide, in-depth investigation which is also quick and cheap. In each case, it is a question of choosing the lesser of two evils.
(2) Because ADR is a voluntary process, it is not appropriate when one party needs immediate judicial relief by way of an interlocutory injunction.
(3) Likewise, ADR is unlikely to resolve 'non-genuine' disputes, for example where a defendant is clearly stalling for time and refusing to admit liability simply in order to hang on to his money for as long as possible.
(4) ADR is not appropriate in 'test cases' where you want a binding, judicial precedent, for example the correct legal interpretation of a clause in a standard form contract.

11.14 FURTHER READING

Fisher and Ury *Getting to Yes* (Arrow Books, 1997)
Scott *The Skills of Negotiating* (Gower Publishing, 1986)
Halpern *Negotiating Skills* (Blackstone Press, 1992)
Kennedy *Everything is Negotiable* (Arrow Books, 1997)
Williams *Legal Negotiation and Settlement* (West Publishing, WA, 1983)
Foskett *The Law and Practice of Compromise* (Sweet & Maxwell, 1996)
Lax and Sebenius *The Manager as Negotiator: Bargaining for Co-operation and Competitive Gain* (Prentice Hall, 1987)

Chapter 12

ADVOCACY

12.1 INTRODUCTION

In answer to the question 'Are good advocates born or made?', most people would say: 'They're born. Advocacy is not one of those things which can be taught'. Many lawyers would probably say the same. Skilled advocates are seen as being eloquent, articulate, and able to think on their feet: all qualities which at first sight seem to be innate rather than acquired. Undoubtedly, some advocates are more naturally gifted than others, but many of these so-called gifts can be acquired through hard work and practice. Perhaps the worst mistake is to assume that good advocacy is simply a matter of flair, and little else. The advocate who demolishes an opponent's witness in cross-examination rarely achieves this by jumping to his feet and firing off the first thing that comes into his head; a great deal of thought and preparation will have gone into every aspect of the challenge he makes.

This chapter gives a basic introduction to advocacy. For those who wish to practise as advocates, it represents the first stage of a continuous learning process. However, others may never appear before a court as an advocate at any stage of their professional careers. Even so, the skills covered in this chapter will prove useful in any situation where effective oral presentation is required.

Chapter 12 contents
Introduction
Skills
The basics
Opening the case
Examination-in-chief
Cross-examination
Re-examination
Closing the case
Ethical issues
Criminal cases: bail and mitigation
Civil cases: chambers applications
Conclusion
Further reading

12.2 SKILLS

The skills of an advocate divide into oral skills and organisation skills.

12.2.1 Oral skills

Advocates are skilled talkers: this is an obvious point which should never be overlooked. Within the stylised atmosphere of the courtroom the task of the advocate, subject to the rules of professional conduct, is to talk his way to the best result that can be obtained for his client. The three major oral skills are as follows.

Presentation

Every advocate needs to be a good storyteller, especially when he is opening a case on behalf of either the prosecution or the claimant. It is not generally realised that a court may know next to nothing about the facts of the case it is about to try or the issues involved: it therefore needs to be put in the picture in a way which will engage its interest.

Argument

Every advocate also needs to be a good persuader. Much of an advocate's time will be spent addressing the court with a view to persuading it to find in favour of his client. Argument may be as to the overall issue of guilt or liability, or as to a subsidiary issue such as bail, the grant of an interim order, or a point of law.

Questioning witnesses

The questioning of witnesses is the skill which young advocates tend to find the most complex and difficult to master. English trials are characterised not only by their adversarial nature but also by the fact that much evidence is still given orally. The ability to extract the relevant evidence from your own witnesses by means of examination-in-chief and to challenge the testimony of an opponent's witnesses in cross-examination is still seen as the most important attribute of the experienced advocate.

In the course of a civil or criminal trial, all three of the above skills will be exercised, but in many other situations, advocacy will consist almost exclusively of presentation and argument. This is particularly true of the vast majority of chambers applications in civil cases, because evidence will almost invariably be given by witness statements. Bail applications and pleas in mitigation in criminal cases also involve very little questioning of witnesses.

12.2.2 Organisation skills

In addition to the oral skills, a good advocate also draws upon other back-up skills which are exercised outside the court room. When an experienced advocate is performing in court, it all seems effortless: he has all the facts at his fingertips, nothing seems to throw him off his stride, and witnesses are examined and cross-examined incisively and in a logical sequence. On top of this, he manages to maintain the appearance of being calm and dignified at the most crucial moments, and never loses his temper. At all times, he is courteous to the court, his opponent, and the most recalcitrant witnesses. To the uninitiated it may look easy, but this level of competence is achieved only by hard work and experience. It is also dependent upon the advocate having thoroughly prepared and organised the case beforehand.

The most important organisation skills are set out below: there is nothing magical about any of them, in fact some of them may appear positively mundane, but no advocate can do without them.

Fact gathering and analysis

No advocate can begin to prepare a case until he has thoroughly mastered its facts. Until this is done, it is impossible to analyse its strengths and weaknesses. Ignorance of the facts will also make it far more difficult to perform adequately in court. For example, when cross-examining a witness it will often be necessary to fire a sequence of rapid questions in order to try and shake his testimony. The task will be made immeasurably easier if the advocate's mastery of the facts is such that there is little or no need to refer to prepared notes before proceeding to the next question. Many readers will have seen US courtroom dramas on television in which advocates never use notes. In real life they are trained to memorise the whole case file. Although UK courtroom style is very different, advocates should try to rely on notes as little as possible.

Knowledge of the relevant law

It is essential to research the relevant substantive law. The advocate must also develop a detailed knowledge of the law of evidence and the relevant procedural law. So far as evidence is concerned, it will always be necessary to study the relevant facts carefully in order to analyse:

(1) what the issues are;
(2) which issues are in dispute;
(3) who has the burden of proof; and
(4) what admissible evidence is available to prove or disprove those issues.

However, that is not enough; you will also need to memorise as much of the law of evidence as you can since an evidential problem may arise unpredictably during the course of a trial. Advocates rarely have time to look the law up in advance of raising an objection.

Similarly, procedural points have a habit of cropping up unexpectedly: an advocate's effectiveness will be greatly enhanced if his level of knowledge is such that these can be identified as soon as they arise.

Handling paperwork

In some respects, handling paperwork is the most neglected organisation skill of all, but it is in fact one of the most important, especially in civil cases. Even quite simple cases can end up producing masses of papers, some of which may need to be referred to at some time during a case. It is important therefore not only to devise a system which enables a required document to be located at a moment's notice, but also to know the contents of every document. This is particularly vital in chambers applications in civil proceedings so far as witness statements are concerned. The master or district judge may intervene by suddenly asking a question on a particular issue. The advocate should immediately be able to refer him to the relevant paragraph in the appropriate witness statements.

The ability to handle paperwork is also assuming a far greater importance in civil trial advocacy with rules requiring pre-trial exchange of witness statements.

12.3 THE BASICS

This section contains a simple checklist to assist in preparation of a case. It also deals with wider aspects of court behaviour and protocol.

12.3.1 Preparation

Good advocacy depends on planning and preparation at every stage. In particular, the order in which you address each task needs to be carefully considered so as to achieve the maximum benefit. The following checklist should always be followed.

Master the relevant facts

If the facts are simple, try to commit them to memory. In more complicated cases, prepare a written chronology for reference purposes which should ideally then be memorised as far as possible.

Analyse the facts

By applying the appropriate substantive, evidential and procedural law you should be able to identify the following:

(1) the legal issues in dispute. Consider in this context whether there are any submissions you will need to make, for example as to admissibility;

(2) the factual issues in dispute. Identify what findings of fact the court will have to make if your client's case is to succeed;

(3) develop a 'theory' of the case consistent with your client's instructions. The more plausible the case advanced, the more likely it is to succeed.

Based upon the analysis above, plan objectives for each stage at which you will be called upon to speak or examine witnesses.

12.3.2 Presentation

Although presentation has been categorised as a specific oral skill, every aspect of the advocate's courtroom role in effect involves conducting a presentation, not only of the client's case but also of the advocate himself. The following list sets out a number of presentational rules which should always be followed.

(1) Maintain eye contact with the person whom you are addressing.
(2) Never read from a prepared text.
(3) Be aware of 'body language'. The way in which an advocate behaves can affect the court's perceptions of his case. Try always to bear the following points in mind:

   (a) Stand still. Advocates who are nervous have a tendency to sway from side to side.
   (b) Stand up straight when in open court. Make sure you know your case well enough to avoid frequent references to your papers.
   (c) Do not speak with your hands in front of your face. This is another common mannerism when a speaker is nervous. Be especially conscious of this trait in chambers proceedings where advocates remain seated.
   (d) Keep your hands and arms still (within reason). Although arm and hand gestures can sometimes be an effective means of emphasising a point they should be used sparingly.
   (e) Keep your emotions under control. To be an effective advocate you will need to be able to hide all kinds of feelings. For example, never appear shocked because a witness says the opposite to what you expect. Learn to sail on unperturbed through the most stormy waters.

(4) Speak slowly in a clear, low tone. If you are anxious, you are likely to speak quickly and in a high voice. In particular, always 'watch the judge's pen'. You are hardly likely to be persuasive if the court cannot keep up with you. The same rule applies when taking the court through documents: it takes time for them to read them and digest their contents.

(5) Do not be afraid of pauses. What may seem to the advocate to be a long gap in presentation is often not even noticed by the court.

(6) Avoid being long-winded and unnecessarily repetitive. These are both traits which suggest that you have not prepared the case very well.

(7) Know your court. All your planning must be with a view to persuading the court of the strength of your case. It is perhaps obvious but nevertheless important to

realise that, for example, a judge will need to be addressed differently from a lay magistrate. Tailor your style to suit your audience.

(8) Be honest and courteous. At all times, bear in mind the need to build and maintain your reputation with the court. The advocate who loses the court's trust is of no use to his client. Always be scrupulously courteous to the court and to your opponent, even if you are disappointed with the way your case has gone.

12.3.3 How to address the court

Nothing reveals an advocate's lack of experience more than a failure to adopt the correct mode of address. The following list should therefore be committed to memory:

Court	Mode of address
High Court Judge:	'My Lord' or 'My Lady' as appropriate
Circuit Judge:	'Your Honour'
Recorder:	'Your Honour'
District Judge of the High Court or County Court:	'Sir' or 'Madam' as appropriate
District Judge of the magistrates' court	'Sir' or 'Madam' as appropriate
Master of the Supreme Court:	'Master'
Supreme Court Costs Judge:	'Master'
Magistrates (lay and stipendiary):	'Sir' or 'Madam' as appropriate.

In the magistrates' court, 'Your worships' is technically incorrect, but frequently used and indeed preferred by many lay benches.

A particular problem is whether it is appropriate to address the court in the second person singular ('You'). In the case of district judges, masters and magistrates, it is perfectly permissible provided 'Sir' or 'Madam' is interposed at appropriate intervals. For example, in a plea in mitigation to a bench of lay magistrates it would be perfectly appropriate to proceed as follows:

> 'Madam, there are three matters relating to the defendant's involvement in these offences that I would like to draw to the attention of you and your colleagues. First, madam, there are two specific aspects of the pre-sentence report which I would like to refer you to…'.

High Court and circuit judges pose more of a problem. As a general rule, 'you' should be substituted by 'Your Lordship(s)', 'Your Ladyship(s)' or 'Your Honour(s)' as the case may be. For example, in the Crown Court before a circuit judge, the previous address would begin:

> 'May it please Your Honour, there are three matters relating to the defendant's involvement in these offences that I would respectfully draw to Your Honour's attention. First, Your Honour, if I might be permitted to draw Your Honour's attention to two specific aspects of the pre-sentence report…'.

To those who are unfamiliar with courtroom protocol, this version may sound unnecessarily obsequious. Nevertheless, this is the level of courtesy expected and you depart from it at your peril. The odd 'you' or 'your' here and there may be acceptable, but do not take risks until you are experienced and know your court.

12.3.4 How to refer to your opponent

It is equally important to extend all the appropriate courtesies to your opposing advocates. Choose from 'My friend' or 'The prosecution/defence' or 'Mr/Ms/Mrs/Miss Smith'. The term 'My learned friend' is traditionally reserved for barristers, although this is no longer a hard and fast rule. If you are opening the case you should always ascertain the name of your opponent since it is a normal courtesy to introduce them to the court. For example: 'Sir, my name is Mr Jones and I appear to prosecute this case and my friend Ms Smith appears on behalf of the defendant'.

12.3.5 Three golden rules when addressing the court

As well as knowing how to behave in court, an advocate must be able to create an impression of being experienced. Failure to observe the following will tend to reveal precisely the opposite.

(1) Do not give evidence yourself

Not only is this improper, it also suggests over-involvement in the client's case. Avoid phrases such as, 'My client tells me ...' or 'I happen to know that ...'. However, it will often be necessary to put the client's views to the court, for example in a civil chambers application or a plea in mitigation in a criminal case. In chambers applications, the phrases, 'I am instructed that', and 'my instructions are', are perfectly acceptable, but in criminal cases they are sometimes interpreted as being coded messages that the advocate does not believe a word the client is saying. Phrases such as, 'I have discussed this with my client and he wants you to know' or, 'My client wishes me to inform you,' are more appropriate.

(2) Do not give your opinion

Avoid using phrases such as, 'In my opinion ...' or 'I think ...'. When an advocate wishes to persuade the court to adopt his view of the case, phrases like, 'I submit,' or, 'I would seek to persuade you,' or, 'I would urge you,' are more appropriate. The important thing to remember is: the only opinion that counts is that of the court.

(3) Object rarely, but quickly

There is an enormous temptation, especially when you have thoroughly researched a case, to object at every opportunity. Indeed, this often impresses the client. However, it will not endear an advocate to the court unless the point is one of substance. Do not object unless the point advances your case or diminishes that of your opponent. Be alert: the decision to raise an objection will often be a split-second one, especially if it involves the issue of whether an inadmissible question has been put to a witness.

12.3.6 Five golden rules when questioning witnesses

Although the examination of a witness is as much an art as a science, the following are basic rules for questioning witnesses which apply whatever the nature of the proceedings.

(1) Keep your questions short

Formulate questions so that, ideally, they do not exceed ten words. If the question is convoluted there is a risk that neither the witness nor the court will be able to follow it. Nothing takes the wind out of an advocate's sails more than being asked to repeat or re-phrase a question because it is incomprehensible.

(2) Ask one question at a time

For reasons similar to those given above, it is essential to refrain from asking multiple questions. The last thing you want is for your opponent to rise to his feet and say, 'Madam, I wonder if my friend would be kind enough to indicate to the witness which question he wants him to answer first'.

This means that a quite simple point may often need to be broken down into several questions before it can effectively be put to a witness. For example, if you are seeking to extract a concession from an identification witness that she was standing 50 feet away, it was dark and it was raining, etc, you may need to ask a whole series of short questions in order to succeed in this objective.

(3) Know your objectives in respect of each witness

This applies as much to your own witnesses as to those of your opponent, but is particularly important when planning a cross-examination.

(4) Try to avoid asking questions in cross-examination to which you do not know the answer

This rule should not be taken too literally because sometimes one has no choice but to probe. The main thing is to ensure that you are never floored by the unexpected. For example, let us assume that you are cross-examining an identification witness on the issue of where she was standing at the time of the incident. If you were simply to ask 'Where were you standing?', you would have no control over the answer. Contrast:

- Q. You said earlier that you were standing on the corner of Main Street and Underwood Road, didn't you?
- A. Yes.
- Q. And there's no dispute, is there, that that is about 50 feet from the incident you say you saw?

Even if the witness says 'No', you have much more control over where to proceed from there. Alternatively, if you can easily prove that the witness was standing 50 feet away, you could quite safely ask the question 'Where were you standing?' because you know that if the witness were to reply 'About 6 feet away', you would have plenty of ammunition with which to contradict her.

(5) Know when to stop

There is always a danger in going on for too long, but it is particularly important not to fall into the trap of asking one question too many. It is a great temptation to press on when you have a witness 'on the run'. However, that is the time to pause and reflect briefly upon whether, having secured some favourable concession, it might not be wiser to refrain from cross-examining further.

For example, if you have managed to extract from the identification witness referred to above concessions that she was standing 50 feet away, it was dark and it was raining, it is a great temptation to then say with a final flourish: 'So how can you be so sure it was the accused that you saw?'

This is the one question you (and your client) may live to regret!

12.3.7 Witnesses: court formalities

There are a number of matters of court protocol concerning witnesses of which you need to be aware, especially since it will be your task to explain them to your client and other witnesses before they give evidence.

Criminal cases

In a criminal case, witnesses other than the defendant should be asked to stay out of court until called.

If the defendant is to give evidence, he must be called before other defence witnesses.

Witnesses may refresh their memories from their written statements prior to being called to give evidence. Other parties must be informed if this has taken place.

Civil cases

In a civil case, witnesses may sit in court throughout the hearing. If the advocate wishes to exclude witnesses from court, he must apply for an order to that effect.

The claimant and defendant are both usually called first by their advocate.

Witnesses may refresh their memories from their written statements prior to being called to give evidence. Other parties must be informed if this has taken place.

12.4 OPENING THE CASE

This section considers opening speeches in all types of proceedings. Although the length and purpose of such speeches may vary widely, they are all vitally important. They provide the advocate with an opportunity to make the first impression. This can be vital, as the court or tribunal may know little or nothing about the case they are about to try. For example, in a criminal trial before magistrates, the bench will probably know nothing about the case other than details of the charges.

12.4.1 Criminal trials in the magistrates' court

The prosecution always has the right to make an opening speech before calling its evidence. In simple trials, this right is sometimes waived. If the prosecutor does open, he will usually:

(1) introduce himself and his opponent to the court;
(2) take the bench briefly through the charges;
(3) outline the facts of the case and the evidence that he intends to adduce in order to prove the charges; and
(4) explain the law, where necessary.

The opening speech requires the advocate to be a good storyteller so that the relevant incidents are brought to life. If there is an item of evidence for which admissibility is in dispute, the prosecutor should make no mention of it when opening, leaving admissibility to be determined at a later stage.

Defence advocates rarely make an opening speech before calling their evidence, because by doing so they lose the right to make a closing speech. Since the prosecutor has no right to a closing speech, the defence advocate will usually take advantage of having the last word.

Apart from the right to make speeches, either advocate may at any stage make a submission on a point of law. In particular, the defence may submit that there is no case to answer at the close of the prosecution case. In such an event, the opposing advocate always has a right to reply.

12.4.2 Civil trials

The claimant's advocate has the right to open (unless, unusually, the burden of proof of all issues lies on the defendant). As judges now have power to dispense with opening speeches, their use may decline, but the practice of handing in a written 'skeleton argument' to the judge in lieu of an opening speech is likely to increase. As in criminal cases in the magistrates' court, if the defendant's advocate elects to make an opening speech, he is not entitled to make a closing speech except with leave of the court.

The purposes of the advocate's opening speech in a civil trial will be to:

(1) introduce himself and his opponent to the court;
(2) indicate the nature of his claim, for example: 'Your Honour, this is a claim for damages for breach of contract';
(3) summarise the areas of dispute between the parties;
(4) outline by reference to the statements of case the alleged facts of the case (nothing which cannot be proved should be asserted), indicating areas of dispute;
(5) introduce the evidence, including any matters contained in agreed documents;
(6) summarise the legal principles involved, indicating areas where a ruling will have to be made.

12.5 EXAMINATION-IN-CHIEF

Examination-in-chief is in many respects more difficult than cross-examination because an advocate should always be seeking to succeed on the strengths of his own case rather than the weaknesses of his opponent's. Accordingly, the way your own witnesses give their evidence has a vital bearing on the overall impression that your case creates in the mind of the court.

12.5.1 The characteristics of examination-in-chief

Although, with one exception, advocates have a complete discretion as to the order in which witnesses are called, it is usual in civil cases for the claimant or defendant, as appropriate, to be called first. In criminal cases, the prosecutor will usually call the victim first, but the defence advocate is obliged to call the defendant before other witnesses as to fact unless the court directs otherwise (Police and Criminal Evidence Act 1984, s 79). The advocate calling the witness will, as a matter of courtesy, begin by announcing each witness in turn, for example, 'Your Honour, I now call the claimant, Margaret Brown'.

The principal objectives of examination-in-chief are:

(1) to present the witness's evidence in a logical sequence (usually chronological or by topic);
(2) to cover all the relevant issues upon which the witness is able to testify; and
(3) to anticipate matters likely to be raised in cross-examination.

The major characteristic of examination-in-chief (and what makes it so difficult for the advocate) is that the witness must, so far as possible, be left to tell his own story with minimal prompting from the advocate. In order to achieve this objective, leading questions are not generally permitted, neither will the witness normally be allowed to refer to any previous written statement made by him (unless it qualifies as a contemporaneous note).

Although there is a degree of controversy over what constitutes a leading question, the generally accepted definition is that it is a question which suggests its own answer by seeking to put words into the witness's mouth. For example, if an advocate was seeking to establish that a witness saw the defendant, James Smith, in The Mitre public house at midday on Monday 21 August (all of which is in dispute), it would not be permissible to ask: 'Did you see James Smith in The Mitre public house at midday on Monday 21 August?'

Instead, the advocate would need to proceed by means of a number of non-leading questions as follows:

> Q. Can you remember what you were doing on Monday 21 August? (This question is arguably leading, but probably not objectionable.)
> A. Well, let me see. Oh yes, I went into work in the usual way.
> Q. Did you stay there all day? (Non-leading)
> A. No, I went out for an early lunch.
> Q. About what time was that? (Non-leading)
> A. Oh, about ten to twelve I think.
> Q. And where did you go? (Non-leading)
> A. A pub called The Mitre.
> Q. Did you see anyone there you recognised? (Non-leading)
> A. Yes, I saw James Smith ...

and so on. As can be readily appreciated this technique requires the advocate to prepare very carefully in advance to ensure that he is able to guide the witness through his evidence without resorting to prompting.

The technique also requires stamina, since it may take time even to elicit a simple set of facts in this way. The only three occasions on which leading questions are permitted by way of exception are:

(1) when the witness's evidence relates to a matter that is not in dispute;
(2) where a denial is invited from the witness; and
(3) on those rare occasions when a witness is declared to be hostile.

An example of exception (1) above would arise if the only dispute was as to the date on which the witness saw James Smith:

> Q. Do you recall an occasion when you saw James Smith in The Mitre public house? (Leading, but not disputed)
> A. Yes.

Q. And can you remember when that was? (Non-leading)
A. Yes, it was on Monday 21 August.

The advocate should always check in advance with his opponent as to what matters can be led to the witness. Matters such as name, address and occupation may always be led, but some advocates prefer to ask witnesses to state these details in their own words to help put them at their ease.

An example of exception (2) would be if Mr Smith's advocate was seeking to extract a denial from his client. It would then be permissible to proceed as follows:

Q. Mr Smith, were you in The Mitre on Monday 21 August at midday? (leading)
A. No, I was not.

Exception (3), namely the hostile witness, is rarely encountered. It is considered in outline only.

12.5.2 The witness who does not come up to proof

Criminal cases

If the witness displays an unwillingness to tell the truth at the instance of the party calling him, the court may declare the witness to be hostile. This allows the advocate who has called him to ask leading questions and, with leave, any previous inconsistent statement made by the witness may be put to him. Such a statement may be used only to discredit the witness's testimony: it is not independently admissible. Further discussion of this difficult technique is not appropriate at this stage.

In most cases, however, the witness's failure to say what the advocate is hoping for is the result of forgetfulness, incompetent examination-in-chief or a poorly taken statement. In such a situation, witnesses cannot be cross-examined. The advocate can only try to repair the damage by calling additional evidence which supports his case. The problem of the forgetful witness may also be avoided if a contemporaneous note of his earlier evidence is available (see **12.5.4**).

Civil cases

The position of the hostile witness in civil cases is broadly similar to that in criminal cases, with one major exception: the court can be invited to treat any previous inconsistent statement as admissible evidence in its own right and, if appropriate, prefer it to the witness's oral evidence (Civil Evidence Act 1968, s 3).

If the witness is not declared hostile, the advocate's options are limited in the same way as in criminal cases (but see **12.5.4**).

12.5.3 Exchange of witness statements

The exchange of witness statements in civil proceedings has made a fundamental difference to examination-in-chief. If a party has served a witness statement and wishes to rely at trial on that witness's evidence, the party must call that witness to give oral evidence unless the court orders to the contrary. The witness's statement will stand as his evidence-in-chief unless the court orders otherwise. This means, in cases involving exchange of witness statements, that examination-in-chief has been reduced to:

(1) formally calling the witness and establishing his name and address;
(2) asking the witness to identify his statement; and
(3) asking the witness whether the contents of the statement are true.

12.5.4 Introducing documents and real evidence

Documentary evidence may be introduced for a variety of reasons. The term 'document' includes items such as photographs, tape-recordings, video films and computer data. From an evidential point of view, it is important to remember not only that a document's authenticity must be established but also that its contents must be admissible for the purpose for which they are tendered. The rules differ materially in criminal and civil proceedings.

Criminal cases

A witness must normally be called to prove the authenticity of any document which is to be adduced in evidence. Although documents cannot be agreed (contrast the position in civil cases), in practice many documents, such as agreed plans of traffic accidents, are routinely admitted. Copies of the documents are generally sufficient (see Criminal Justice Act 1988, s 27). A police officer will normally be called to prove the authenticity of a defendant's written confession. This will be done by asking the officer to identify the defendant's signature and recount the circumstances in which the statement was made. If accepted, the original will be admitted as an exhibit. The police officer will then normally be invited to read the defendant's written confession to the court. Although most interviews with suspects are now tape-recorded, the written summary of the interview will basically be proved in the same way.

The other commonly encountered document is the 'contemporaneous note'. The basic rule is that a witness may, with leave of the court, refresh his memory in the witness box from any document which was made or verified by him substantially contemporaneously with the events to which he testifies.

Police officers, in particular, will frequently ask for leave to refresh their memories from notes contained in their pocket books, but other witnesses may also be permitted to refer to their original statements.

The advocate conducting the examination-in-chief will question the witness in order to establish whether the document falls within the rules. The opposing advocate may then cross-examine the witness solely on that issue. Only after leave has been granted will any further evidence-in-chief be given by the witness. The opposing advocate is entitled to inspect the document and may cross-examine the witness about its contents, subject to certain technical rules which are outside the scope of this chapter. Although witnesses are not otherwise allowed to refer to their written statements in the witness box, the court does have a discretion to allow a witness to leave the witness box to read his statement (*R v Da Silva* [1990] 1 All ER 29). When the witness resumes giving evidence, it must be given orally without further reference to the statement.

Real evidence consisting of other objects, for example a weapon, must likewise be proved by a witness who can show that they are what they purport to be and that they are relevant to the issues. It will also be necessary to prove that an appropriate chain exists which links the object to the defendant.

Civil cases

In theory, a witness must be called on to prove the authenticity and originality of each document which is to be adduced in evidence. However, in civil cases, documents are almost invariably agreed. They will usually be put in as one or more agreed bundles by the claimant's advocate in the course of his opening speech. Furthermore, the use of documents is inextricably bound up with the rules as to disclosure, expert evidence and exchange of witness statements, all of which are outside the scope of this chapter.

The rules relating to the use of contemporaneous notes to refresh the memory and the court's discretion to allow the witness to leave the witness box to read his statement are the same as in criminal cases. These rules have effectively been overridden in cases where there are exchanged witness statements.

12.6 CROSS-EXAMINATION

Effective cross-examination is generally regarded as representing the highest level of advocacy. The skilled advocate, by harrying his opponent's witnesses with probing questions, can effectively demolish the other side's case. However, it is an art hedged with misconceptions, most of which derive from watching too many fictional courtroom dramas. The aggressive language and sarcastic manner that are characteristic of the television soap opera are usually inappropriate in the real world.

Cross-examination is a vast topic which deserves a book to itself (many such books have been written over the years). It is also a skill which requires constant practice. The basic principles can be stated fairly briefly, but detailed examination is outside the scope of this chapter.

12.6.1 Defining objectives

Advocates should always give careful thought to what they hope to achieve by cross-examination. In order to do this effectively, it will be necessary to develop a 'theory' of the client's case. This theory should be a plausible version of the events, consistent with the available evidence and the client's instructions which, if accepted, will result in the court finding in the client's favour. Once the advocate has developed this theory, he will find it easier to work out his tactics.

Another point to be borne in mind is that, whatever tactics are to be adopted, the cross-examining advocate must always 'put his case' to his opponent's witnesses. In other words, the advocate must confront his opponent's witnesses with all aspects of the client's case which conflict with their evidence. This need not be done directly. One often hears advocates saying, 'I put it to you that ...' as if it were an essential ritualistic device. However, it is possible to be more subtle than this. For example, using the illustration in **12.5**, if Mr Smith's advocate needed to put to the witness that it was in fact on 22 August that he saw his client in The Mitre, it would be permissible, but inadvisable, simply to state: 'I put it to you that you are mistaken, it was on 22 not 21 August that you saw Mr Smith in The Mitre, wasn't it?'

If the answer were to be 'No', that would be the end of the matter.

Suppose, however, that the cross-examining advocate knew that the witness regularly went to The Mitre at that time: the client's case could be expressed more effectively in the following way:

Q. It's true, isn't it, that you regularly go to The Mitre for lunch?
A. Yes.
Q. At about the same time each day?
A. Yes.
Q. Around midday?
A. Yes.

The cross-examiner could continue by trying to establish that there was nothing special about 21 August, before suggesting to the witness that he had in fact got the day wrong and that he had seen the defendant on a different day.

In other respects, the cross-examiner has considerable freedom of manoeuvre in deciding how to structure his cross-examination. There are four main questions to consider.

(1) Should I cross-examine at all?

It may well be that unless the advocate needs to put the client's case, it is better to ask no questions at all. This is especially so if a witness has not directly damaged the case. Cross-examination may increase the risk of eliciting unfavourable material that would otherwise not come out.

(2) Are there any favourable matters that I can extract?

It is far better for an advocate to get a witness on his side, than to confront him. For example, in a case involving disputed identification, try gently to elicit concessions from the witness that it was, for example, dark and raining at the time, rather than suggest aggressively that his evidence is worthless.

(3) Is there any way in which I can discredit the witness's evidence?

Witnesses can, and often do, make mistakes or erroneous assumptions that can be exposed by cross-examination. Very few witnesses deliberately give false evidence. This always needs to be borne in mind when probing for weaknesses. Again, an indirect rather than a confrontational approach is likely to yield better results. Exposing inconsistencies by reference to a previous inconsistent statement is a particularly effective method. It is governed by special legal rules which are outside the scope of this chapter.

(4) Is there any way in which I can discredit the witness himself?

It is rare for the advocate to find himself in a position to insinuate, for example, that the witness is biased. It is a particularly risky tactic when done on behalf of a defendant in a criminal trial because of the dangers of falling foul of the Criminal Evidence Act 1898, s 1(3)(ii). In any case, the tactic should never be adopted unless there is independent evidence available to substantiate the allegations.

The above four questions are not mutually exclusive: a cross-examining advocate may wish to adopt those parts of a witness's testimony which favour his client whilst challenging other parts which do not. This is a highly skilled and complex operation.

12.6.2 The technique of cross-examination

The major difference between examination-in-chief and cross-examination is that the advocate cross-examining is permitted to ask leading questions. This is a particularly valuable right since it enables him to retain tighter control of the witness than is the case with non-leading questions. However, leading questions should not be used to excess since this may give the impression that the witness is being brow-beaten. The tactic can, however, be particularly effective when an advocate wishes to expose inconsistencies or illogicalities. The trap can be set by asking the witness a series of non-leading questions on peripheral matters as a preliminary to confronting him with weaknesses or inconsistencies in his testimony by means of a series of tightly controlled leading questions. This is a highly skilled exercise.

Two general examples will suffice. Suppose that you were trying to discredit the testimony of an identification witness. There would no doubt be a number of matters which you had thoroughly researched beforehand, such as where he was standing, how far away he was from the incident, the time of day, the weather conditions, etc. You would no doubt wish to keep tight control of this part of your cross-examination by means of leading questions. However, it might also be appropriate to probe into what the witness had been doing beforehand by means of non-leading questions. For example, you might ask: 'Now Mr Smith, you say you were on your way home when you witnessed this incident; where were you coming from?'

The answer might be: 'I'd been down The Mitre for a drink'.

Not all cross-examinations will yield such promising results, but it can be seen that much useful information can be gleaned from peripheral matters by means of non-leading questions without running any risk to one's case.

A second example might be in the case of a witness whom an advocate wished to confront with a previous inconsistent statement. It might be appropriate to begin by inducing him by means of non-leading questions to embellish his story still further before confronting him with his inconsistencies. This is a particularly effective technique where the allegation is that the witness is biased.

12.7 RE-EXAMINATION

Once cross-examination is completed, the advocate who called the witness has the right to re-examine. That right is limited in that: first, he may deal only with matters raised in cross-examination; and secondly, leading questions are not permitted. Very few advocates are skilled re-examiners. It is a sophisticated art. As a general rule, it is most unwise to re-examine unless you are absolutely certain as to your objectives. Its principal function is to repair any damage done in cross-examination, by giving the witness an opportunity to explain or qualify his previous answers. It is useful where, for example:

(1) cross-examination has confused the witness;
(2) the cross-examiner has attempted to impeach the witness's credit;
(3) the cross-examiner has elicited only partial details of an incident which appears to favour the opponent's case.

12.8 CLOSING THE CASE

Closing a case can be more difficult than opening, because a greater degree of improvisation is required. An opening speech can be worked out in detail beforehand: by the time an advocate rises to make a closing address, all the evidence will be before the court and the case may look very different by then. However, it is rare that the central issues will have changed, only the details. It is absolutely vital, therefore, to have identified the likely issues and evolved a 'theory' of the case in advance. It is only in this way that a closing address can deal with all the outstanding issues in a coherent and persuasive manner. It is important to remember that, just as the advocate who opens the case has the advantage of the first word, so the closing speaker is the last advocate the court will hear before retiring to consider its verdict.

12.8.1 Who closes the case?

Criminal cases

The basic rule in magistrates' court trials is that only the defence will make a closing speech. The only exception is in those rare cases where the defence has both opted to make an opening speech before calling its evidence and been given leave to make a closing speech. In such a case, the prosecution is also permitted to make a closing speech, but the defence will still address the court last.

Civil cases

Except where the defendant began or where the defendant calls no evidence, the advocate for the claimant has the last word in a civil case. If the judge says that he does not wish to hear a closing speech, then the claimant has probably already won.

12.8.2 The purpose of the closing speech

Criminal cases

Be brief. Magistrates' courts are very busy places and you will be well advised to confine yourself to the essential points which advance your client's case. However, the experienced advocate will not allow himself to be rushed. If you need a few moments to compose yourself and go over your notes, do not hesitate to ask for them. You should always cover:

(1) any relevant points of law;
(2) the key issues in dispute;
(3) any part of the evidence which weakens the prosecution case and strengthens that of the defence.

Avoid saying too much about the burden and standard of proof. Magistrates need little reminding of this. It is better to concentrate on those parts of the evidence which genuinely raise a reasonable doubt.

Civil cases

The position in civil cases is broadly similar to that in criminal cases, except that an advocate must always be aware that he is addressing a judge, not magistrates. Modify your style accordingly. Since civil trials still take place on the statements of case, a closing speech which follows the issues raised by the statements of case will greatly assist the court. Judges are particularly grateful to advocates who not only summarise the issues that are still outstanding but also emphasise the essential findings of fact which the judge will have to make in order to decide the case.

12.9 ETHICAL ISSUES

An advocate's reputation with the court is his most valuable asset. An advocate who has lost the court's trust through some piece of unethical conduct is a liability. All advocates should be familiar with the Law Society's Code for Advocacy (see *The Guide to the Professional Conduct of Solicitors* (The Law Society, 1999), p 385).

12.9.1 Criminal cases

Duties of the prosecution advocate

The duties of the prosecution advocate are:

(1) to ensure that all relevant facts and law are before the court;
(2) to make available to the defence any evidence which is inconsistent with the evidence which a prosecution witness gives at the trial.

Duties of the defence advocate

The duties of the defence advocate are:

(1) to say on a client's behalf all that the client would properly say for himself;
(2) to keep confidential all information received about a client and his affairs which the client wishes to keep confidential;
(3) to ensure that the prosecution discharges the onus placed upon it to prove the guilt of the accused. The defence advocate is entitled to put the prosecution to proof even if the defendant has admitted his guilt;
(4) to disclose to the prosecution and to the court all relevant cases and statutory provisions relating to the case, even if unfavourable to the defence. However, unfavourable evidence need not be disclosed;
(5) not to participate in a positive deception of the court. A solicitor may not continue to act for a client who misleads the court (eg by giving a false name, or giving evidence which the advocate knows to be untrue) unless the client is prepared to reveal the truth;
(6) not to act for two or more clients whose interests are in conflict, even if invited to do so by the court.

12.9.2 Civil cases

Advocates for the claimant and the defendant are bound by the same rules which are:

(1) to ensure that all relevant facts and law are before the court;
(2) to say on a client's behalf all that the client would say properly for himself;
(3) to keep confidential all information received about a client and his affairs which the client wishes to keep confidential;
(4) where relevant, to ensure that the opponent discharges the onus placed upon him by the burden of proof;
(5) to disclose to the court all relevant cases and statutory provisions relevant to the case, even if not favourable to the client. The advocate may then seek to show that decisions which are against him are erroneous, not binding, per incuriam, or

distinguishable. As in criminal cases, the theory is that unfavourable evidence need not be disclosed. However, the rules as to disclosure and exchange of witness statements are such that, in practice, both parties may be required to disclose such evidence;

(6) not to participate in a positive deception of the court. A solicitor may not continue to act for a client who misleads the court (eg by giving evidence which the advocate knows to be untrue) unless the client is now prepared to reveal the truth;

(7) not to act for two or more clients whose interests are in conflict.

12.10 CRIMINAL CASES: BAIL AND MITIGATION

A detailed study of criminal advocacy in bail applications and pleas in mitigation is outside the scope of this chapter. However, a very basic guide to the skills required is set out below. Because most criminal advocates will begin their careers with a simple bail application or plea, it is often erroneously assumed that this is 'easy' advocacy. Nothing could be further from the truth: there is nothing easy about a situation in which the client may face a period in custody if his advocate fails him.

12.10.1 Bail

The skills of the advocate will be required only when the application is opposed. Although bail is always ultimately a matter for the court, it will normally be granted as a matter of course unless the prosecution objects. Since defendants have a right to bail prior to conviction, it is customary for the Crown Prosecutor to begin by formally setting out his objections by reference to the prescribed criteria in the Bail Act 1976, Sch 1, Pt I. The objections will almost invariably be based on an assertion that there are substantial grounds for believing that the defendant will either abscond and/or commit further offences while he is on bail. The risk of the defendant interfering with witnesses is also frequently advanced as an objection.

The task of the defence advocate is twofold. First, he should seek to put forward arguments which tend to minimise the risks adverted by the Crown Prosecutor. Thus, for example, if the prosecution claims that there is a substantial risk of the defendant absconding, this might be rebutted by arguing that:

(1) the defendant is pleading not guilty and the evidence against him is weak;
(2) the defendant's record (if he has one) reveals that he has never absconded whilst on bail in the past;
(3) even if he is convicted, the likelihood of a custodial sentence is remote.

These are very general illustrations: each case must be dealt with on its own facts. Whatever the facts, thorough preparation is always essential.

Secondly, the advocate must neutralise any substantial risks by putting forward a sensible package of conditions, such as a surety combined with a condition of residence, which will be sufficient to persuade the bench that they can afford to take a risk and grant bail. Although the Bail Act 1976, s 4 is supposed to secure a right to bail, in reality if a prosecutor raises substantial grounds for withholding bail the defence advocate has a difficult task upholding that right. An effective application, therefore, requires as much advance preparation as the circumstances permit. The Crown Prosecution Service (CPS) should always be approached (in advance if practicable) in order to obtain as much information as possible about both the offence and the defendant.

If possible, you should obtain detailed instructions from the client concerning his personal circumstances and the existence of any potential sureties. It may be that this will avoid a contested application altogether. If you can produce an appropriate package of conditions to the CPS before the hearing, you may be able to persuade them to withdraw their objections. So far as the actual application itself is concerned, an advocate should always bear three things in mind.

(1) Structure the application in such a way that each prosecution objection is countered in a logical sequence, and conclude with any package of conditions you wish to put forward.
(2) Keep the application as short as circumstances permit and remember that courts usually have a long list of cases to hear.
(3) Tailor the application to the individual client. Magistrates are often offered the same platitudes whatever the nature of the application such as: 'My client strenuously denies the charge, has a fixed address and instructs me that he has been offered work on a building site'.

The statement may be true, but it is vitally important to interest the court in your client's personal circumstances. It might therefore be more appropriate to explain a little more about why your client's denial is so significant. For example:

> 'Sir, if I might begin by referring you to the case against Mr Smith, you will see that it is tenuous in the extreme. The evidence consists solely of hotly disputed identification evidence' ... and so on.

12.10.2 Pleas in mitigation

As with bail applications, advance preparation is essential. Courts can sentence only on the basis of information and, although the sentencing court may have a written pre-sentence report (PSR) available (this is mandatory when the court is considering a custodial sentence or certain types of community penalty), there will often be a great deal of further relevant background information which the defence advocate can put before the court. The Criminal Justice Act 1991 places the seriousness of the offence at the forefront of the matters to which the court must have regard when passing sentence. Nevertheless, the court is not precluded from considering the circumstances of the individual offender by way of mitigation. A useful starting-point in the magistrates' court is to consult the Magistrates' Association Sentencing Guidelines.

The following eight points should always be considered when preparing a plea.

(1) Thoroughly research the realistic sentencing options available, referring, where appropriate, to relevant statutory or judicial guidelines.
(2) Take as full a written statement as possible from the client, dealing with the circumstances both of the offence and of the client.
(3) Obtain an up-to-date copy of the client's criminal record, and deal thoroughly with the circumstances of any offences which the court may regard as being 'aggravating' within the Criminal Justice Act 1991, s 29(2).
(4) If a PSR has been ordered, try to contact the Probation Service in advance of the case to see if they will discuss its contents informally.

(5) Arrive at court in plenty of time so that you can discuss your mitigation speech with the client and obtain his approval of your proposed course.
(6) When called upon to address the court, invite them to read any PSR first.
(7) When the court has read the PSR, begin your speech by dealing with matters which affect the seriousness of the offence. Then go on to deal with matters of offender mitigation, referring where appropriate to the PSR. Never read paragraphs of the PSR aloud, because the document is confidential. Instead, invite the court to consider the appropriate paragraph. For example: 'Madam, you will recall that Mr Smith's family history is dealt with at the top of page 2 of the pre-sentence report. I would particularly draw your attention to the matters dealt with in paragraph 3 ...', and so on.
(8) Conclude by 'showing the court the way home'. In other words, if you can suggest a realistic sentencing option which the court can take, you are not only discharging your duty to the client, but also assisting the court. Sentencing an offender is never easy, and anything which helps the court discharge this onerous duty will be gratefully received.

12.11 CIVIL CASES: CHAMBERS APPLICATIONS

12.11.1 Key characteristics

It is particularly important to master the skills relevant to chambers advocacy in civil cases, because trainee solicitors have full rights of audience. A chambers application is any application made to the court after the proceedings have been commenced and before the trial of the action. In the High Court, those chambers applications requiring a hearing will be dealt with by a master (in the central office in London) or a district judge (in the district registry). In the county court, these will be dealt with by a district judge. All chambers applications, whether in the High Court or the county court, share a number of common features.

(1) There are no 'live' witnesses. With rare exceptions, all the evidence will be in witness statement form. Hence the principal tasks of the advocate are to present his case and to argue for the order sought.
(2) Advocates are seated (except for some applications before a master).
(3) The proceedings are heard in public (unless the court otherwise directs).

12.11.2 Preparing for the application

Although the subject-matter of an application may vary considerably from case to case, there are a number of steps which should always be taken.

(1) Try to agree as much as possible in advance.
(2) Make sure all relevant witness statements are served before the hearing. Although the court may be prepared to accept a late witness statement, it will result in your client being penalised in costs.
(3) Make sure that you have mastered the facts of the case and that you are familiar with the contents of the statements of case and witness statements. You may find it useful to prepare a written chronology of the case including the key events and steps in the action from issue of proceedings to date. It is not uncommon for the master or district judge to deal only with those particular points in the case which he considers need arguing. Your grasp of the facts and documentation therefore needs to be such that you can locate them instantly. If

the case is a complex one consider handing to the master or district judge a written chronology which you have agreed with your opponent.

(4) The master or district judge should have a copy of the court file. However, you will need to ensure that you have copies of any relevant documents to hand to the master or district judge, should the court file be incomplete.

(5) Prepare brief notes. Although you should never read out your submissions, it will help you to have a list which sets out the points that you intend to raise. Focus on the main facts to be addressed. You might use a highlighter pen on copy documents (not the originals) for this purpose. Write in the margin of a copy witness statement a brief summary of what each paragraph contains. An example of such a note in a contract case might be: 'Para 3 – Summarises the dispute as to time of delivery'.

(6) Make sure you have read and flagged the relevant passages in the Civil Procedure Rules 1998 and Practice Directions.

(7) Have a very clear idea of the order you want the master or district judge to make. If you are making the application, you should attach to the application notice a draft of the order you propose (except in the most simple applications).

(8) Work out in advance any relevant interest calculation and costs order the master or district judge is likely to make. Also consider whether the master or district judge should make any directions for the future conduct of the action.

(9) Consider the prospect of an appeal should your application be unsuccessful. An application for permission to appeal may be made to the master or district judge at the end of the hearing.

12.11.3 Conducting the application

Whether the claimant or the defendant is the applicant, the party whose application it is will begin. The order of speaking will be the same whether the proceedings are in the High Court or the county court.

The applicant's case

If you are representing the applicant, the procedure is as follows.

(1) FORMALLY INTRODUCE YOURSELF AND YOUR OPPONENT AND IDENTIFY ANY RELEVANT DOCUMENT ON THE COURT FILE TO WHICH YOU INTEND TO REFER

For example:

> 'Good morning, sir, my name is Mr Holtam and I am from Collaws. I represent the claimant, David Mills. Miss Gibson, from Evans and Co, represents the defendant.
>
> The claimant's application today is for summary judgment.'

You should then check that the district judge has all the documents you intend to refer to on the court file and ask if he has read them.

The master or district judge will not have copies of the correspondence between the parties or their solicitors. You should refer to such correspondence only if it is exhibited to a witness statement.

(2) BY REFERENCE TO THE DOCUMENTS, CONCISELY IDENTIFY THE ISSUES (LEGAL AND FACTUAL) FOR THE COURT TO DECIDE AND HIGHLIGHT THE RELEVANT FACTS

State the issues clearly before taking the master or district judge through the documents. Argue for the order sought on the basis of the issues you have identified from the documents.

Take the master or district judge through the documents at a sufficiently slow pace to enable him to digest their contents. It is not normally necessary to read them out verbatim; you should merely refer to paragraphs and summarise their effect. If the master or district judge has read the papers, your summary can be quite concise. More detail is needed where the papers have not been read. Refer to any exhibits in a way which ties them in with and explains the contents of the relevant witness statement. You do not need to refer to matters that are not in dispute between the parties.

If your opponent is present, you should have asked him before the hearing whether he wishes to take the court through his witness statement himself or whether he is happy for you to do this.

Anticipate and deal with all disputed matters revealed by your opponent's evidence.

(3) SUCCINCTLY REFER TO THE RELEVANT LAW AND/OR PROCEDURE

Explain simply which Rule you are relying on and apply it to the facts of the case.

(4) CONCLUDE SUBMISSIONS FOR THE ORDER SOUGHT

Emphasise what you consider to be your best points and explain briefly why you are entitled to the order sought. Be prepared to address the court on an alternative or 'second best' order if you think the court is not prepared to grant the order you really want.

If you are applying for summary judgment, the master or district judge will expect an interest calculation.

Make it clear to the master or district judge that you have finished your application. For example: 'Sir, unless I can help you further, that concludes my application'.

The respondent's case

The respondent's case will be structured differently as the court will by now have been taken through all the evidence. None the less, the respondent's case follows a similar model.

(1) SO FAR AS NECESSARY, IDENTIFY ANY RELEVANT DOCUMENT ON THE COURT FILE TO WHICH YOU INTEND TO REFER

The applicant should have introduced you and therefore there is no need for you to introduce yourself again. If the applicant failed to introduce you, then you should introduce yourself.

You should identify the documents that you will be relying on as a basis for your response, for example:

> 'Sir, in opposing this application I will be relying on the Defence and the Defendant's witness statement.'

(2) BY REFERENCE TO THE DOCUMENTS, CONCISELY IDENTIFY AND DEAL WITH ISSUES (LEGAL AND FACTUAL) FOR THE COURT TO DECIDE, HIGHLIGHT RELEVANT FACTS AND ADDRESS APPLICANT'S SUBMISSIONS

You should identify what you want the court to do and why.

The applicant has already taken the master or district judge through the statements of case and the evidence. Take the master or district judge to the relevant paragraphs in the statements of case and the witness statements which support your arguments. Present a positive case in support of your opposition to the order sought by the applicant. Do not just reply to the points made by the applicant. After presenting your positive case, deal with each of the applicant's points, however difficult it is to do so. Stress the effects of making the order on the action and, if it be the case, that the application is an attempt to blur the real issues and/or to prevent them being properly decided by the court after hearing oral evidence.

(3) SUCCINCTLY COUNTER THE APPLICANT'S ARGUMENTS ON THE RELEVANT LAW AND/OR PROCEDURE

Reply to the legal points raised by the applicant. Distinguish, if possible, the applicant's authorities and introduce any you rely on.

(4) CONCLUDE SUBMISSIONS AGAINST THE ORDER SOUGHT

Briefly emphasise why the order requested by the applicant should not be made (or at least, if it is made, why it should only be in modified form).

Make it clear to the master or district judge that you have finished your opposition. For example: 'Sir, unless I can assist you further, those are the grounds upon which I oppose the order sought'.

The applicant's final word

The master or district judge will normally invite the applicant to respond to matters raised by the respondent.

The applicant should deal with the points made against him preferably in the same order in which they were put. This can be done very briefly if it is a point which has already been dealt with by the applicant earlier. If it is a new point, face it squarely and be quick to point to any evidence or document that supports your assertions. Encapsulate why the court should make the order you seek.

In some cases, it may be appropriate for the applicant simply to state:

> 'Sir, in my submission, my friend's arguments wholly fail to meet the case that I put before you. Accordingly, Sir, unless there are any matters that you wish me to deal with I do not propose to address you further other than to ask respectfully that you grant the order as sought.'

Closing the case

The master or district judge then gives a reasoned judgment and writes his order in note form on the court file. This indorsement forms the basis for the order subsequently drawn up.

If appropriate, the master or district judge will give directions for the further conduct of the action. Be prepared to ask for any directions which you feel are necessary.

The party who has won usually asks for costs, and the loser is given the opportunity to reply. Be prepared to make submissions on the appropriate costs order and why.

Appeals

At the end of the hearing, the master or district judge may ask the parties if they wish to appeal his decision. An application for permission to appeal may be made to the master or district judge at the hearing. Permission to appeal may be given only where the court considers that the appeal would have a real prospect of success or there is some other compelling reason why the appeal should be heard.

Effective chambers advocacy

Although the subject-matter and nature of chambers applications cover an enormous range, it is vitally important for the advocate to make his submissions as clearly and concisely as possible in order to help the court, especially since it hears so many applications during a working day.

12.12 CONCLUSION

Although this chapter could not deal in detail with the subject, it has provided an introduction to some of the salient features of the advocate's art. It should also have made clear the fact that many of the skills of the advocate can be acquired through study and observation. Remember that thorough preparation is the key: without that, no advocate can be fully effective – however fluent his oral skills may be.

12.13 FURTHER READING

Evans *Advocacy in Court* (Blackstone Press, 1995)
Napley *The Technique of Persuasion* (Sweet & Maxwell, 1991)
Monkman *The Technique of Advocacy* (Butterworth Law, 1991)
Murphy and Barnard *Evidence and Advocacy* (Blackstone Press, 1998)
The Guide to the Professional Conduct of Solicitors (The Law Society, 1999)

INDEX

References are to paragraph numbers.

Addressee
    adapting style for   1.3
Advising, *see* Interview
Advocacy   9.1, 12.1 *et seq*
    argument, skill of   12.2.1
    bail applications   12.10.1
    body language   12.3.2
    closing speech   12.8
    conflict of interest, and   12.9.1, 12.9.2
    court, addressing   12.3.3, 12.3.5
    cross-examination   12.6
    ethical issues   12.9
    evidence
        advocate not to give   12.3.5
        admissible, knowledge of   12.2.2
    examination-in-chief   12.5
    facts
        analysis of   12.2.2, 12.3.1
        gathering   12.2.2, 12.3.1
    mitigation, plea in   12.10.2
    modes of address   12.3.3, 12.3.4
    objections   12.3.5
    opening speeches   12.4
    opinion   12.3.5
    opponent, reference to   12.3.4
    oral skills   12.2.1, 12.3.2
    organisation   12.2.2
    paperwork handling   12.2.2
    preparation   12.2.2, 12.3.1
        checklist for   12.3.1
        key to effectiveness   12.12
    presentation, rules for   12.2.1, 12.3.2
    questioning witnesses   12.2.1, 12.3.6, 12.5.1,
        see also Witness
    research of relevant law   12.2.2
    rules of conduct
        civil cases, in   12.9.2
        criminal cases, in   12.9.1
    strengths and weaknesses of case, analysis of   12.2.2
    trial, *see* Civil case; Criminal case
Advocate
    born or made   12.1
    civil case, in   12.9.2, *see also* Advocacy; Civil case
    criminal case
        duties in   12.9.1
        see also Advocacy; Criminal case
All England Law Reports   4.2.1, 4.2.2, 6.5.4
    consolidated tables and index   4.2.2
Alternative dispute resolution   11.13
    advantages of   11.13.2
    cheapness   11.13.2, 11.13.3
    disadvantages of   11.13.3
    meaning   11.13.1
    speed of   11.13.2, 11.13.3
Analysis
    legal, skill of   2.2.2
Attendance notes   1.4.2
Attestation clause   1.2.3

Bail
    application for   12.10.1
Bargaining
    negotiation, in   11.9.2
BATNA
    negotiation and   11.5.4, 11.5.5, 11.9.2
        consideration of possible alternative courses   11.5.4
Body language
    advocate, of   12.3.2
    interpretation of   9.4
    own   9.4, 10.4.1
Books
    practitioner's   3.2, 5.1.4
        examples   3.2
        loose-leaf   3.2, 5.1.2
        statutory material in   4.1.4, 5.1.2
        supplements   3.2
        use of   2.4, 3.2, 5.1
    precedents, of   3.2
Brussels Merger Treaty   6.2.1
Butterworths Direct   7.3.4

CD-ROM
    advantages and disadvantages   7.1.2
    Current Law Citators on   5.3.2
    information on   5.3.2, 5.4.1, 5.4.2, 7.1.1, 7.2.1
    use   7.1.1, 7.1.2, 7.1.3, 7.2.2
Case-law
    citations   4.2.2
    Current Law Citator   5.3.2, 7.2.1
    databases of   7.2.1
    European   6.5, *see also* European Community law
    Law Reports, The, *see* Law Reports, The
    names   4.2.2
    reports   4.2, *see also* Law reports
    research into   4.1.4, 5.2, *see also Current Law*; LEXIS
CELEX   7.2.1
Chambers advocacy   12.11.1, *see also* Civil case
Chambers applications   12.11, *see also* Civil case

Citation
    case-law 4.2.1
    European secondary legislation, of 6.3.2
    UK statutes, of 4.1.2
Civil case
    see also Advocacy
    chambers application 12.11
        appeals 12.11.3
        applicant begins and ends 12.11.3
        chronology, preparation of 12.11.2
        closing of case 12.11.3
        conduct of 12.11.3
        costs 12.11.3
        features 12.11.1
        filing of affidavits 12.11.2
        High Court or county court,
            in 12.11.1, 12.11.3
        order required, clear idea of 12.11.2
        preparing for 12.11.2
        procedure in 12.11.3
        respondent's case 12.11.3
        service, when proof needed 12.11.3
        time periods, interest calculations, etc,
            preparation for 12.11.2, 12.11.3
    closing 12.8, 12.8.1
        approach to 12.8.2
    documentary evidence in 12.5.4
    opening speech 12.4.2
    order of speeches 12.4.2
    rules of conduct 12.9.2
    statements of case 12.11.3
    witness, order of 12.5.1, see also Witness
    witness statements 12.11.3
Civil Procedure Rules 1998 12.11.2
Client
    attendance at negotiating meetings 11.6
    care of, Law Society's
        recommendations 10.5.8
    instructions from 2.2.1, 10.5.7, see also
        Interview
    misleading court 12.9.1, 12.9.2
    needs of 2.2.4
    types of, writing style for 1.3.1
Commencement
    statute, of 4.1.4, 5.1.2, 5.1.3
Commencement Order 5.1.2
Communication 9.1
    interviewing, skills in, see Interview
    non-verbal 9.4
    oral, see Oral communication skills
    questioning, see Questions
Compact disk 6.6, 7.1.1
Computer
    data, as evidence 12.5.4
    use of, as electronic library 7.1.1
Correspondence
    medium for negotiation, as 11.12
    skills, see Letter writing

Cost
    case, of, for client 10.5.4, 10.5.8
        discussion of, approach to 10.5.8
        information to be given 10.5.8
        time to broach 10.5.4, 10.5.8
    interview, of 10.5.4
County court
    chambers applications 12.11, see also Civil
        case
Court
    addressing, rules for 12.3.3, 12.3.5
Criminal cases
    see also Advocacy
    bail applications 12.10.1
    closing 12.8, 12.8.1
        approach to 12.8.2
    documentary evidence in 12.5.4
    magistrates' court, in 12.4.1
    mitigation, plea in 12.10.2
    opening speech 12.4.1
    order of speeches 12.4.1
    rules of conduct 12.9.1
    witness, order of 12.5.1, see also Witness
Crown Prosecution Service 12.10.1
Current Law 5.3
    Case Citator 4.2.2, 5.3.2
        updating 5.3.3
    CD-ROM, Citators on 5.3.2, 7.2.1
    law report citation abbreviations in 4.2.1
    European references 6.3.7
    Legislation Citator 4.1.2, 4.1.4, 5.3.2
        updating 5.3.3
    monthly digests 4.1.4, 4.2.1, 5.3.3
    Statutes 5.1.2, 5.3.1, 5.3.2
    statutory instruments in 5.1.4, 5.3.2
    updating, use for 4.1.4, 5.3
    Year Book 4.1.4

Daily Law Reports Index 4.1.4, 4.2.2, 5.4.2
Daily List 5.1.2
Database 7.1.1
    European legislation, of 6.6
    LAWTEL, see LAWTEL
    LEXIS, see LEXIS
Deed
    execution clause in 1.2.3
Defence
    bail application 12.10.1
    duties of advocate 12.9.1, see also Advocacy
    plea in mitigation 12.10.2
Defendant
    evidence from 12.3.7
Definitions
    Act, in 4.1.4
    use of, in documents 1.2.5

Delegated legislation
    sources of (UK)   4.1.3, *see also* Statutory instrument
Directives, *see* European Community law
Document
    see also Drafting; Legal document
    meaning   12.5.4
Draft
    amendment to other side's   1.2.8
Drafting   1.2 *et seq*
    see also Style
    ambiguity   1.2.7
    blanks   1.2.7
    checking   1.2.4
    clause construction   1.2.5
        Coode, George, structuring clause according to   1.2.5
    copy of drafts, good practice   1.2.8
    definitions   1.2.5
    discretion, creating   1.2.7
    ejusdem generis rule   1.2.7
    ethical considerations   1.2.8
    further reading   1.5
    language   1.2.7
    obligation, creating   1.2.7
    passive, verbs in   1.2.7
    planning   1.2.6
    practical considerations   1.2.8
    precedents, use of   1.1.2, 1.2.6, 3.2
    presentation   1.2.5
    preliminary steps   1.2.1
    revising   1.2.6
    structure, points on   1.2.2, 1.2.3

E-mail   7.9
Ejusdem generis rule   1.2.7
Electronic library   7.1–7.3
    see also CD-ROM; LEXIS
    databases available   5.4, 7.7.2
Ethics
    advocacy, and   12.9
    drafting, and   1.2.8
    negotiation, and   11.3, 11.5.3
European Atomic Energy Community   6.2.1
European Coal and Steel Community   6.2.1
European Commission   6.3.1, 6.4.4, 6.5.3
    website   7.3.2
European Community law
    case-law   6.5
        All England Law Reports series   6.5.4
        CELEX, on   6.6, 7.2.1
        citation   6.5.2
        courts   6.5.1
        European Court Monitor   6.5.3
        law reports   6.5.3, 6.6
        LEXIS, on   7.3.2
        proposals, information on   6.4.2
        translation   6.5.3
    Council of Ministers   6.3.1
    courts   6.5.1
    Current Law, references in   6.3.7, 6.5.3
    Decisions   6.3
    Directives   6.3
        binding force of   6.3.1
        incorporation into UK law   6.3.6
    draft legislation
        European Access, use of   6.4.2
        Official Journal, in   6.4.3
        tracing   6.4.1
        up-to-date information on   6.4.4
    Encyclopedia of   6.3.4
    Financial Times European service   6.4.4
    Halsbury's Laws volumes   3.3.3, 6.3.7, 6.5.3
    law reports   6.5.3
    legislation
        database of   6.6
        draft, *see* draft legislation *above*
        primary, *see* primary legislation *below*
        secondary, *see* secondary legislation *below*
    LEXIS, on   7.3.2
    Official Journal, The   6.4.3, 6.5.3
    Opinions   6.3.1
    primary legislation   6.2.1
        sources   6.2.2
    proposals   6.1, 6.4
    Recommendations   6.3.1
    Regulations   6.3
    research into
        general   6.1.1
        library sources   6.1.2
        starting point   6.1.3
    secondary legislation   6.3.1, 6.3.2
        checking status of   6.3.5
        citation   6.3.2
        incorporation of Directives into law, checking   6.3.6
        keeping up-to-date, sources for   6.3.5, 6.3.7
        sources   6.3.3, 6.3.4, 6.3.7
        tracing   6.3.4
    Treaties, founding EC   6.2.1
        texts of   6.2.2, 6.6
European Court Monitor   6.5.3
European Court of First Instance   6.5.1, 6.5.2
European Court of Justice   6.5.1, 6.5.2, 6.6
European Economic Community   6.2.1
European Parliament   6.4.4
Evidence
    admissible
        dispute as to   12.4.1
        investigation of   12.2.2
    alternative dispute resolution, and   11.13.3
    defendant, from   12.3.7
    documentary   12.4.2, 12.5.4
        scope of   12.5.4

Evidence *cont*
    objects, etc, as   12.5.4
    unfavourable, disclosure of   12.9.1, 12.9.2
    witnesses, *see* Witness
Examination-in-chief   12.5
    exchange of witness statements, effect
        on   12.5.3
    written statement standing as   12.5.3
Execution clause   1.2.3

Foreign law
    see also European Community law
Forum
    negotiation, for   11.12

Green Form scheme   10.5.4
Ghosting letters   1.3.2

Halsbury's Laws of England   2.4, 3.1, 3.3
    Abridgment volumes   3.3.4
    cases, search for   4.2.2
    Consolidated Index   3.3.1, 3.3.5
    Current Service   3.3.4, 3.3.5
        index   3.3.4
    diagram for use of   3.3.5
    Digest   4.2.1
    European Community law volumes   3.3.5, 6.3.7
    main volumes   3.3.2, 3.3.5
    monthly reviews   3.3.4, 3.3.5
    Monthly Update   3.3.4, 3.3.5
    Noter-up   3.3.4, 3.3.5
    searching in   3.3, 4.2.2
        summary   3.3.5
    updating method   3.3.4
    User's Guide   3.3
Halsbury's Statutes   5.1.2, 5.1.3
    citations, as source of   4.1.2
    commencement of Acts   5.1.2, 5.1.3
    components of   5.1.3
    Cumulative Supplement   5.1.3
    Current Statutes Service   5.1.2, 5.1.3
    European legislation in   6.2.2
    General Index   4.1.2, 5.1.3
    Is It In Force?   5.1.2, 5.1.3
    Noter-up   4.1.2, 5.1.3
    Table of Statutes and General Index   4.1.2, 5.1.3
    updating of   5.1.2
    using, guidance on   5.1.3
Halsbury's Statutory Instruments   5.1.2, 5.1.5
    commencement orders, list in   5.1.2
    components of   5.1.5
    Cumulative Supplement   5.1.5

    Monthly Survey   5.1.5
    texts in   5.1.4, 5.1.5
    updating service   5.1.5
    using, guidance on   5.1.5
Hansard   4.1.4
    CD-ROM, on   7.2.1
High Court
    chambers applications   12.11, *see also* Civil case

Information
    client, from   2.2.1, *see also* Interview
    client, to   10.5.8, 10.6.2
    confidentiality, advocate's duty   12.9.1, 12.9.2
    revealing, to other side   11.5.3
Internet sources   7.1.2, 7.3.6
Interview
    advising in   10.3.2, 10.4.4, 10.5.7
    analysis of problem   10.4.3
    body language   10.4.1
    care of client   10.5.8
    checklist   10.4.2, 10.5.1
    closing   10.3.2, 10.5.8
    costs, dealing with   10.5.4, 10.5.8
        estimate of   10.5.8
    details, ascertaining   10.3.2, 10.4.2, 10.4.5, 10.5.6
    discussing options   10.5.7
    environment of   10.3.2, 10.5.1
    explanation to client   10.4.4
    facts, obtaining   10.3.2, 10.5.5
    failings   10.2
    feelings of client   10.4.1, 10.4.2
    first impressions   10.5.1, 10.5.3
    follow-up tasks   10.5.8
    further reading   10.6
    Green Form scheme   10.5.4
    greeting   10.5.3
    information gathering   10.4.2, 10.5.1
    inhibitions of client   10.4.2
    interruptions, freedom from   10.5.1
    Law Society recommendations   10.5.8
    legal aid   10.5.4, 10.6.2
    legal position, explaining   10.4.4, 10.5.7
    listening   9.2, 10.3.1, 10.4.1, 10.5.5
    model for   10.3.2, 10.5.2
    notes of   10.3.2, 10.4.5
    objectives of   10.1
    obstacles created by solicitor   10.2
    opening   10.5.3–10.5.5
    parting   10.5.9
    plan of campaign from   10.5.7
    preliminaries   10.5.4
    preparing for   10.3.2, 10.5.1
    questions   9.3, 10.4.2
        closed, uses   10.4.2

Interview *cont*
    questions *cont*
        leading   9.3.2, 10.4.2
        open, uses   10.4.2
        'T-funnel'   10.4.2, 10.5.6
    record of   10.3.2, 10.4.5
    research, prior to   2.2.1
    seating   10.5.1
    silences   10.4.1
    skills required   9.1–9.4, 10.3.1, 10.4, 10.5.4–10.5.8
    structure of   10.3.2
    summarising   10.4.2, 10.5.6
    thinking time   10.4.2, 10.4.3
    time frame for case, indication of   10.5.8
    timetable for   10.3.2, 10.5.4

Jargon
    avoidance of   1.2.7, 10.4.4, 10.5.7
Journals   5.1.2, 5.4, 7.2.1
    law reports in   4.2.1
    Legal Journals Index   5.4.1
Judges
    mode of address   12.3.3
Judicial decisions, *see* Case-law
Judicial review   4.2.2
JUSTIS   7.2.1

Law reports   4.2.1
    abbreviations   4.2.1
    citation   4.2.1
    Daily Law Reports Index   4.1.4, 4.2.2, ¨ 5.4.2
    European cases, for   6.5.3
    index to, using   4.2.2
    journals, in   4.2.1
    legal periodicals, in   4.2.1
    newspapers, in   4.2.1
    official   4.2.1
    specialist   4.2.1
Law Reports, The   4.2.1
    CD-ROM, on   7.2.1
    Index to Digest of Cases   4.2.2
        LAWTEL   7.3.5
Layout   1.2.5, 1.4.1
Legal aid   10.5.4, 10.6.2
Legal document
    clause construction   1.2.5
    drafting, *see* Drafting
    structure of   1.2.3
Legal drafting, *see* Drafting
Legal periodicals
    commencement orders in   5.1.2
    law reports, in   4.2.1
Legal research
    academic and practical distinguished   2.1
    advocate, by   12.2.2
    assembling facts   2.2.1
    assumptions on, in book   2.3
    case-law, on, *see* Case-law
    client's instructions prior to   2.2.1
    Current Law, use of, *see Current Law*
    developments, checking   2.6.2, *see also* updating *below*
    electronics materials, through use of   7.1 *et seq*
    European law, into, *see* European Community law
    foreign law, into   7.3.2
    further reading   2.7
    Halsbury's Laws, use of   2.4, *see also Halsbury's Laws*
    Halsbury's Statutes, use of, *see Halsbury's Statutes*
    Halsbury's Statutory Instruments, use of, *see Halsbury's Statutory Instruments*
    index of sources, use   2.5.2
    key point extraction   2.4, 8.2
    legal analysis   2.2.2, 10.4.3
    legislative materials, on   4.1, 5.1, *see also* Statute; Statutory instrument
    library use   2.2.3, 2.4, *see also* Library
    organisation of   2.4
    report   2.4, 8.2
        aims   8.2
    results
        communicating   2.4, 8.2
        recording   2.4, 2.6.3, 8.2
    sources   2.4, 2.5
        categories of   4.1
        general or particular   2.3
    subject index, use   2.5.1
    textbooks, in, *see* Books
    updating   2.6, 3.1, 3.2
        notes made during   2.4, 2.6.3, 8.2
Legalese
    avoidance of   1.2.7, 1.3.1, 10.4.4, 10.5.7
Legislative material
    citation and use   4.1
    collections of   5.1
    delegated legislation, *see* Statutory instrument
    developments, ensuring check on   5.1.1, 5.3.3, 5.4
    statutes, *see* Statute
Letter writing   1.3 *et seq*
    addressee, adaptation for   1.3.1
    beginnings and endings   1.3.3
    checks before posting   1.3.5
    content   1.3.4
    final checks   1.3.5
    ghosting   1.3.2
    overall structure   1.3.4
    second thoughts   1.3.5
LEXIS   7.3.2
    statutes   5.1.2

LEXIS cont
   statutory instruments 5.1.4
Library
   European Community law, sources of 6.1.2
   use of
      see also Books; *Halsbury's Laws of England*
      assumptions on, in book 3.1
      skills 2.2.3, 2.4
Listening
   encouraging speaker, signals 9.2.1
   importance of 9.2
   interviews, in 10.3.1, 10.4.1, 10.5.5
   negotiating meeting, in 11.8.3
   summarising, uses of 9.2.2, 10.4.2

Maastricht Treaty 6.2.1, 6.2.2
Magistrates
   mode of address 12.3.3
Meeting
   negotiation, for 11.6, 11.12
      attendance at 11.6.4
      purpose and agenda 11.6.6, 11.6.7
      time for 11.6.1
      venue, length, seating, etc 11.6.2–11.6.5
      see also Negotiation
Memoranda
   approach to writing 1.4.2
Mitigation
   plea in 12.10.2

Negotiation 11.1 *et seq*
   aggression 11.4.6
   agreement
      authority for 11.11.5
      reaching 11.2, 11.4.5, 11.10.3
      'zone' for 11.5.6
   aims 11.2
   alternative dispute resolution, see Alternative
      dispute resolution
   assertiveness 11.4.1, 11.4.2, 11.4.6
   bargaining 11.7, 11.9.2
   best alternative to a negotiated agreement
      (BATNA) 11.5.4, 11.5.5, 11.9.2
   client's position, looking behind 11.5.2
   closing 11.8
      agreement, after 11.10.3
      means of 11.10.2
      timing 11.10.1
   collaboration 11.4.6
   competitiveness 11.4.5, 11.9.2
   compromise, use of 11.4.4, 11.5.5, 11.9.2
   concessions 11.9.2, 11.10.2
   co-operativeness 11.4.1, 11.4.2
   correspondence, by 11.12
   deadlines 11.10.2
   false 11.11.4
   deadlocks 11.9.4
   definition 11.2
   discussion during 11.7, 11.9.1
   dispute resolution, as 11.1, 11.13
   ethical aspects of 11.3, 11.5.3
   expert, independent, use of 11.9.1
   feinting 11.11.3
   flexibility in 11.2, 11.4.7
   forum for 11.12
   further reading 11.14
   issues and priorities 11.5.5
   knowledge of law, facts and procedure, need for
      11.5.1
   lying 11.11.8
   meetings, at 11.6, 11.12
      see also other entries above and below
      adjournment 11.9.3, 11.11.1
      preparation for 11.6
      strategy 11.6.8, 11.8–11.10
      use 11.12
   misrepresentation 11.5.3
   notes 11.9.2, 11.12
   opening 11.7
      'aiming high' 11.5.5
      climate for 11.8.1
      ground rules, host's duty 11.8.2
      party to start 11.6.9
      'resistance point' 11.5.5
   opening bid 11.5.5, 11.6.9, 11.8.3
   opening statement
      general rules 11.8.3
      importance of 11.8.3
      other side, of 11.8.4
   overview of 11.7
   phases of 11.8–11.10
   planning 11.5.2–11.5.7
   preparation for 11.4, 11.6.10
      importance of 11.5.1
   process of 11.7
   seating 11.6.5, 11.11.7
   settlement zone 11.5.6
   silence, use of 11.9.1, 11.12
   strengths and weaknesses 11.4.7, 11.5.3
   styles 11.4
      charts 11.4.1
   summaries, use of 11.8.4, 11.10.3
   tactics and tricks 11.11
   telephone, by 11.12
   transaction-based 11.1, 11.5.2, 11.5.4
   ultimatum 11.10.2
   underlying interests identifying 11.5.2
   variables, identifying 11.5.5, 11.9.2, 11.9.4
      what variables are 11.5.5
   venue for 11.6.2
Newspapers
   Financial Times European Service 6.4.4
   information for lawyers on CD-ROM 7.2.1

Newspapers *cont*
   law reports in   4.2.1
Non-verbal communication   9.4, 10.4.1
Note
   attendance, of   1.4.2
   'contemporaneous', use of by witness   12.5.4
   interview, made in   10.3.1, 10.4.5
   negotiations, of   11.9.2, 11.12
   record of research, as   2.4, 8.2

Official Journal
   draft legislation in   6.4.3
   orders and judgments, indications of   6.5.3
On-line materials   7.3
Operative part
   legal document, of   1.2.3
Oral communication skills   9.1, 12.1
   advocacy, *see* Advocacy
   ability to use   9.1
   listening, *see* Listening
   practising techniques   9.1
   questions, *see* Questions
   requirement of   9.1
Padding
   avoidance of   1.2.7
Parties
   document, in   1.2.3
Periodicals, *see* Journals
Photograph
   evidence, as   12.5.4
Police officer
   evidence, and   12.5.4
Practitioner works   3.2, 5.1.4, *see also* Books
Precedents
   books of   3.2
   use of   1.1.2, 1.2.6
Probation Service
   informal discussions with   12.10.2
Pre-sentence report   12.10.2
Professional misconduct   11.5.3, 11.11.8,
see also Ethics
Pronoun
   use of   1.2.7
Prosecution
   see also Advocacy
   closing speech, circumstances for   12.8.1
   examination-in-chief, order   12.5.1
   opening speech right to   12.4.1

Questions   9.3
   classification   9.3, 10.4.2
   closed   9.3.2, 10.4.2
      negotiation, use in   11.9.1
   interviews, in   10.3.1, 10.4.2
   leading

      interview, in   9.3.2, 10.4.2
      trial, at   12.5.1, 12.6.2, 12.7
   open   9.3.1, 10.4.2
      negotiation, use in   11.9.1

Recital clause   1.2.3
Record
   attendance note as   1.4.2
   interview, of   10.4.5
   negotiations, of   11.9.2, 11.12
   research, of   2.4, 2.6.3, 8.2
Report
   cases, of, *see* Law reports
   pre-sentence (PSR)   12.10.2
   research, on   2.4, 8.2
   writing, approach to   1.4.1
Research, *see* Legal research

Schedules
   use of   1.2.3
Sentence/clause structure   1.2.5
Sentencing
   plea in mitigation, and   12.10.2
Silence
   interview, use in   10.4.1
   negotiation, use of   11.9.1, 11.12
Solicitor
   advocate, as, *see* Advocacy; Advocate
   charging rates   10.6.2
   communication skills   9.1–9.4
   conducting case, informing client of   10.5.8
   instructions from client   2.2.1, 10.5.7
   interview with client, *see* Interview
   listening skills   9.2
   negotiator, as   11.1, *see also* Negotiation
   Practice Rules on interviews   10.5.8
   trainee, rights of audience   12.11.1
   written skills   1.1.1
Stationery Office
   Act, copy from   5.1.2
   Daily List   5.1.2
   statutory instrument, copy from   5.1.4
      database   7.2.1
Statute
   annotated   5.1.2
   citation   4.1.2
   commencement, checking for   4.1.4, 5.1.2, 5.1.3
   Current Law Citator   5.3.2, *see also* Current Law
   example   4.1.4
   Halsbury's Statutes, *see* Halsbury's Statutes
   finding   5.1.2, 5.1.3
   interpretation   4.1.4
   official copies   5.1.2

Statute *cont*
   sources of   4.1.4, 5.1
   updating on   5.1.2, 5.3.2, 5.3.3, 5.4, *see also*
      LEXIS
Statutory instrument
   citation   4.1.3
   Current Law Citator   5.3.2
   finding   5.1.4, 5.1.5
   procedure for making   4.1.3
   updating on   5.3.3, 5.4
Style
   active and passive verbs   1.2.7
   adjectives and prepositions, use of   1.2.7
   jargon   1.2.7
   layout   1.2.5
   legalese   1.2.7, 10.5.7
   letters, *see* Letter writing
   memoranda, of   1.4.2
   numbering and tabulation   1.2.5
   padding   1.2.7
   paragraphing   1.2.5
   presentation   1.2.5
   report, of   1.4.1
   sentence structure   1.2.7
   unfamiliar words, use of   1.2.7
   word order   1.2.7
Surety
   bail application, in   12.10.1

Tape-recording
   evidence, as   12.5.4
Telephone
   medium for negotiation, as   11.12
Textbooks, *see* Books
Time
   case, for, indication of   10.5.8
   expressions of   1.2.7
Timetable
   interview for   10.3.2, 10.5.4
Treaty
   Brussels Merger   6.2.1
   Maastricht, of   6.2.1
   Paris, of   6.2.1
   Rome, of   6.2.1
Trial
   see also Advocacy; Civil case; Criminal case
   closing speech
      defence and/or prosecution, by   12.8.1
      improvisation required   12.8
      purpose of   12.8.2
   court, addressing
      golden rules for   12.3.5
      modes of address   12.3.3
   opening speeches
      importance of   12.4
      order of   12.4.1, 12.4.2
   witness, examination etc, *see* Witness

Updating, *see* Case-law; LEXIS; Statute; Statutory instrument

Verbiage
   avoidance of   1.2.5
Video film
   evidence, as   12.5.4

Weekly Law Reports   4.2.1, 7.7.2
   Westlaw-UK   7.3.5
Witness
   announcing   12.5.1
   biased   12.6.2
   civil case, in   12.3.7
   contemporaneous note, use of, by   12.3.7, 12.5.2, 12.5.4
   court formalities   12.3.7
   criminal case, in   12.3.7
   cross-examination   12.6
      distinguished from examination-in-chief   12.6.2
      leading questions   12.6.2
      need for   12.6.1
      objectives, defining   12.3.6, 12.6.1
      technique of   12.6.2
   examination-in-chief   12.5
   hostile   12.5.2
   leading questions   12.5.1, 12.6.2, 12.7
   oral evidence   12.5.3
   order of calling   12.5.1
   questioning   10.1, 12.2.1, 12.3.6
      guidance on   12.3.6
   re-examination   12.7
   statements
      exchange of   12.2.2, 12.5.3
      use of   12.5.3, 12.5.4
   weaknesses, probing   12.6.1
Writ   12.11.2, 12.11.3
Writing, *see* Drafting; Letter writing; Report; Style
Written skills
   approach to   1.1.2